DATE DUE

Modern Factoring

Modern Factoring

Irwin Naitove

American Management Association, Inc.

Standard book number: 8144–2127–X
Library of Congress catalog card number: 72–93788

Foreword

FACTORING, in some form, has been with us since the American Revolution. Yet there are some who still say: "Oh, so you're in the factoring business. What does your factory make?"

And there are those who ask: "Factoring . . . what's that?"

Then there are others who smile knowingly, and with an "Oh, yes" response, convey the impression that they know. But very often they really don't. They assume that factoring is associated in some way with outrageous interest rates and shady money-lending practices, that it is a last resort for businesses gasping for their financial lives. This prejudice stems quite naturally from the growth over the years of many small companies that have incorporated the word "factor" into their names. Their operations, however, bear little resemblance to those of the two dozen or so firms historically known as "old-line factors."

Just what is factoring? How does factoring serve modern business?

The substantial, long-established factoring company is, as some definitions of the word "factor" state, "an agent, a doer, a maker," a business-servicing organization equipped to assist growth companies to grow faster. To accomplish this objective, the factoring company provides professional credit approval and collection, as well as complete accounts receivable bookkeeping services. At the same time, the factoring company assumes without recourse its clients' credit risks, and offers business counseling, marketing advice, and a wide variety of management information reports. This is a far cry from the notion held in some quarters that the factor is a side-street, second-string money lender who feeds on the carcasses of dying businesses.

On the contrary, the old-line factoring company is a highly respected, complex, professionally staffed organization serving a wide variety of financially sound firms, many of them publicly held and involved in the manufacture and sale of nationally branded merchandise. For a reasonable charge, clients may buy financial and technical resources far more extensive than they could afford to provide for themselves: the talent, efficiency, experience, and flexible financing techniques that will contribute to the realization of their profit goals.

Commercial factoring has played a vital role in the development of American industry for almost 350 years. In recent years factoring has gone international, and grows steadily in importance as a valuable tool of modern business. Yet too many businessmen, attorneys, accountants, and financial advisers are not as familiar as they might be with its functions and techniques.

In this book we will acquaint company management, financial executives, professional financial advisers, students, and others with the functions and operations of the modern factoring organization. A full understanding of the available services is an essential part of the equipment of those charged with the responsibility for financial and managerial planning.

IRWIN NAITOVE

6

Contents

I

Factoring
in Historical Perspective

On that cold twenty-first day of December in 1620 when the Pilgrims went ashore from the Mayflower to a land "full of woods and thickets," they had an unseen but most important companion. As a matter of fact, it was this "silent partner" who had made it possible for them to sail from Plymouth, England, after three full years of sky-rocketing hope and plummeting despair. It would seem that anyone so important to the beginnings of this nation would merit more than merely a mention, a line, or at most a sentence in the history books. However, this partner was neither flesh nor blood, could not carry a musket or cook food or read a prayer book. Yet there is no doubt that, without him, the Mayflower would never have carried the Pilgrims to their meeting with destiny on the "wild and savage" coastline nearly 350 years ago.

This "silent partner" was what has come to be known as a factor. The arrangements entered into by the Pilgrims with a group of London merchants to finance an expedition to the New World were an early form of factoring, whereby the funds were advanced on collateral for repayment at a maturity in the future.

The roots of factoring go down deep into the business history of America. Not only has factoring grown with the country, it has also made an important contribution to the emergence of the United States from a series of tiny, isolated settlements hugging the Atlantic coast to the most highly industrialized nation in the world.

The Factor and a New Life

With the Plymouth colony established on the shores of the New World, the settlers were faced with the realities of building a fresh life. Their problem was twofold: how to obtain the goods and materials needed to build the colony, and how to retire the debt incurred as a result of the voyage of the Mayflower. It was finally decided that certain men within the colony would form a general partnership to trade in colonial and English merchandise so that the colonists would be able to obtain such items as shoes, cotton and woolen cloth, tools, muskets, and powder and shot, while the partnership would earn sufficient profits to retire all debts. The London merchants with whom the agreement had been made would, in turn, receive and sell all shipments from the colony, primarily animal furs, fish, and timber. In the trading agreement, these London merchants were referred to as "agents and factors."

So the term factor became an integral part of the vocabulary and lives of the early settlers. As the young colonies traveled the arduous road toward independence, the factor progressed with them, serving as personal agent entrusted with the local interests of distant business enterprises.

With the struggle for independence won, the new nation began to take giant strides toward the west. By 1800, Pittsburgh was the far west, and the tiny, isolated settlements were now on the Ohio and Tennessee Rivers. The necessities of life were in ever increasing demand—manufactured goods that could be put to immediate use in the burgeoning cities and on the expanding frontier. Most manufactured goods still came from England and other European countries. And the agent or factor system of distribution, which had originated in the Plymouth colony, had kept pace with the surging country, and was still the primary means by which European merchandise reached the American people in 1800.

In return for a commission, the factor undertook responsibility for the sale of goods, guaranteed the colonial purchaser's credit, and collected the accounts due to the European exporter. At times the factor even provided warehouse facilities. Frequently, merchandise shipped to the American settlements was consigned to the factor before it was sold to the ultimate customer. Since the factor was in a position similar to that of the modern franchised distributor—that is, in direct contact with its customers— it could also provide its European clients with information about the products required by their customers.

Early Concentration in Textiles

In those early days, the selling and merchandising activities of the factor were concerned mainly with textiles.

European mills provided most of the fabrics that the American processor converted into clothing and home furnishings. The factor received these goods on consignment and occasionally made advances to the shipper against the consigned merchandise. It also sold the goods to American processors whose credit it guaranteed. Here, too, if the shipper so desired, the factor would make periodic advances to him against the accounts receivable which were created by the sale of his goods.

Then, as the Industrial Revolution burst upon the youthful American business community, the role of the factor began to undergo marked changes. The clothing and home furnishings manufacturers were building their own plants and creating their own internal sales forces to market their domestic products throughout the country. Their dependence upon the factor for selling and merchandising services disappeared. But as their own salesmen began to develop new market areas, more and more the factor became a specialized banking and credit-servicing organization.

In these circumstances, the mill retained the factor to determine the credit standing of its customers. The factor guaranteed payment by approved customers and purchased its client's accounts receivable outright, without recourse. The customer then made his payment directly to the factor. The factor also advanced funds against the value of the merchandise, which was controlled either by lien or by warehouse receipts.

New Needs for Factoring Services

Many of today's old-line factoring firms trace their origins back to the early or middle years of the 1800's. As the economy of the nation began to change from one dominated by agriculture to one dominated by industry, the old-line factors began to reach out beyond the textile industry. They had accumulated vast amounts of financial data and had developed extensive and sophisticated credit techniques. Throughout the country they could see the emergence of new industries that needed the expert services that they could provide so well. A vacuum was being created; if the factoring firms did not fill this void, then some other existing institutions would—or a new industry would be created to serve the purpose.

Knowing that no industry can stand still, the old-line factors began aggressively to seek out new clients. Their initial overtures were to the clothing and home furnishings manufacturers that had been the customers of the factors' original clients. In this way the factoring house became exposed, not only to the operating peculiarities of the manufacturer, but also to those of department stores, jobbers, and small retailers. In turn, some of these became the factor's clients.

To develop operational information on the activities of these new customers, the factor organized its staff into groups of specialists. Within a single credit department could be found specialists in the affairs of retailers, wholesalers, manufacturers, and importers. The factor amassed great files of detailed credit information, developed specialized bookkeeping and collection techniques, and acted as financial adviser, consultant, and private banker to a broader-than-ever variety of American businesses.

From its early, narrow confines within the textile and apparel industries, factoring has expanded its services, in recent years, to include manufacturers of products for both consumer and industrial markets—for example, sporting goods and toys, automotive accessories, plastics, building materials, and photographic, optical, and communications equipment.

New Forms of Financing

In the early 1900's, while the old-line factors were evolving and refining their techniques for serving American business, a financing phenomenon known as the discount finance company appeared. This newcomer was not concerned with credit guarantee and invoice collection, and did not purchase accounts receivable or assume consumer credit risk. Its sole interest was in financing business. The discount finance company made loans to its clients against the collateral of assigned accounts receivable. The client was provided with a revolving loan. The customer was not informed that the invoices it received were assigned to a third party. If the customer failed to pay the invoices, the loss would be the client's, not the finance company's. As the finance companies extended their operations, they made loans against the collateral of inventory as well as plant and equipment.

When Henry Ford revolutionized the American manufacturing system and unloosed the first mass production society in the history of the world, he also created the problem of how to give the bulk of the American people the power to purchase these products. The solution was a method whereby the ultimate consumer could purchase a product and use it while paying for it over an extended period of time. Soon consumers were purchasing, through installment payments, products they would ordinarily have had to forgo or, at best, could not have purchased without years of saving.

Time-sales purchases, more than anything else, made it

possible for the American consumer to absorb the variety of new products coming off factory assembly lines. Many finance companies entered the installment sales field, advancing funds against contracts involving the sale of pianos, automobiles, and, later, a large variety of durable consumer goods. In some cases, products were handled without notification to the buyer; in other cases, the buyer made his installment payment directly to the finance company. Today, the consumer sales finance company is a basic fact of American economic life.

The formerly sharp dichotomy between the old-line factor and the finance company has been modified by the growth-stimulated need to employ capital and by the competitive pressure on profit margins. Most finance companies now contain factoring divisions that are fully qualified to render credit, bookkeeping, and collection services, and, conversely, most major old-line factors have divisions that lend funds against receivables or other collateral and offer leasing and equipment time-sales facilities.

The factoring/finance companies of today offer a wide range of financial services to a variety of industries. They sell financing and specialized servicing in flexible packages, in most cases tailoring their arrangements to meet each client's needs. By 1968, the commercial financing and factoring industry did a business volume in excess of $26 billion. The magnitude of these figures indicates the significant role that factoring/finance companies play in sustaining a high level of business activity.

Factoring Abroad

Since World War II, the growth of national and international commerce has created a demand for the specialized techniques of factoring in such countries as England, Belgium, France, Holland, West Germany, Italy, Norway, Sweden, Denmark, and Switzerland. Several American factoring companies have formed overseas branches to handle business in foreign countries, while others have established joint ventures with European partners. Factoring facilities have also been established in the Far East.

In some respects, the factoring industry has come full circle. At its inception in colonial days, factoring handled the importing of goods from Europe; then, for a long period of time, the factors concentrated on domestic goods and products; and now, many factoring companies have once again begun to finance and handle the sales of large quantities of merchandise manufactured in Europe and Asia.

There are few national boundaries to contain factoring. Wherever nations are striving to develop their industries and to raise the standard of living of their people, the need for factoring exists. As factoring has gone hand in hand with the development of the American economy, so it can assist the growth of industry throughout the world.

2

The Services
of the Modern Factor

The first thing to realize about a modern factor is that it is, indeed, modern. The picture that sometimes comes to mind, of the shirt-sleeved clerk with the green eyeshade and the paper cuffholders held together by rubberbands, is as outdated as the nineteenth century. The modern factor is a streamlined, departmentalized organization employing the latest and most efficient business procedures and staffed by talented and specialized personnel. The needs of clients served by the factor are so varied that it would be impossible to handle them effectively without such an organization. For operational efficiency, a major factoring house is separated into two basic divisions: the factoring division and the commercial finance division. Let us first examine the factoring division and the services that it renders to clients.

The Factoring Division

Prior to an analysis of specific factoring services, it would be advantageous to define factoring more carefully. Factoring is the outright sale of accounts receivable without recourse. The factor assumes the credit risk and handles all details of collection.

The administration of the factoring division is organized into the following departments:

- Account sales: Records details of client transactions with the factor.
- Credit: Researches and approves (or rejects) the credit risk on all orders submitted by clients before shipment to their customers.
- Collection: Collects outstanding receivables purchased from clients.
- Bookkeeping: Records client invoices; applies and records payments received from customers.
- Accounting: Correlates all transaction data and renders monthly accounting reports to clients.

A more detailed discussion of the functions of these departments is given in the chapters that follow.

The services that the factor performs for the client—credit approval, accounts receivable bookkeeping, and collection—are essential to the client's operation, but they are not the basic areas from which the client creates profit. The growth and profitability of a company are determined primarily by the effectiveness of its research, product development, manufacturing techniques, marketing, and financial management. By placing in the hands of the factor those functions which are not intrinsic to overall profitability, and which can be undertaken with greater skill and efficiency by the factor, the client is free to concentrate both his capital and his talents on the task of strengthening the areas where his profits are earned.

Factoring services are offered in three basic variations:

- Conventional or standard factoring.
- Maturity factoring.
- Maturity factoring with an assignment of equity.

Conventional or standard factoring. This type of factoring is designed for the client whose cash requirements are higher than the amount of funds that he can borrow from a bank on an unsecured basis against balance sheet working capital. This client can obtain the necessary financing from the factor, and receive in addition the services of credit protection, bookkeeping, and accounts receivable collection, which a straight banking relationship cannot provide.

Factoring essentially increases the client's liquidity. To illustrate this point, we list below an example of the balance sheet of a client before and after factoring. Before factoring, the manufacturer of our illustration was unable to avail itself of trade discounts, because its accounts receivable turnover was too slow to allow it to pay its trade payables promptly. In this illustration, you will note that although working capital remains identical, the cash flow speed-up from factoring of receivables permits the client to remain current with suppliers, even though it maintains the same inventory level required by its volume of business. The difference in cash velocity stems from the fact that a factored client literally sells its accounts receivable for cash at the time of shipment and does not have to wait for the customer to remit promptly (or slowly) on the original terms.

Liquidity before factoring:

Cash	$ 21,000		Bank loan	$ 60,000
Accounts receivable	159,000		Accounts payable	120,000
Inventory	180,000		Accruals	45,000
	$360,000			$225,000
Working capital:	$135,000			

Liquidity after factoring:

Cash	$ 5,000		Bank loan	$ –0–
Due from factor	70,000		Accounts payable	75,000
Inventory	180,000		Accruals	45,000
	$255,000			$120,000
Working capital:	$135,000			

The mechanics of conventional factoring are simple and clearcut. The creditworthiness of all orders received from the client are checked by the factor's credit department. When orders are filled and merchandise shipped, the factor purchases the sales invoices, which notify the client's customers that bills are payable directly to the factor. The factor then handles accounts receivable record keeping and collection, and guarantees payment to its client.

In conventional factoring, all the client's billings for the month are computed to a hypothetical average maturity date on which the factor will remit the accumulated funds to the client at no interest charge. However, if the client requires cash advances against these receivables at any time after shipment but before the maturity date, they are available to him on request.

These cash advances are not loans, since they are made against money due to the client at a later date. On the client's balance sheet there is no liability to the factor for funds that have been advanced. On the contrary, the balance of undrawn funds still held by the factor is carried as an asset on the client's financial statement.

Maturity factoring. Maturity factoring involves no financing, only service. The factor provides the client with a credit guarantee for all customers whose orders are approved prior to shipment, thus shielding the client from any bad debt losses. It is then the factor's responsibility to collect the net sales proceeds from customers. On the average due date for each month's sales, the factor turns over the accumulated funds to the client. No interest is charged, since the client has taken no advances against his sales prior to the date when they have theoretically matured and been paid. In fact, the factor remits to the client whether or not he has actually received payment from the clients customers. For all these services, the client pays a fee or service charge computed as a commission on net sales factored.

Actually, the service performed by the factor is reminiscent of that rendered by the old-line factors to their early clients in the textile industry—credit guarantee, receivable bookkeeping, and collection service. Clients who utilize this type of factoring arrangement are usually firms with substantial working capital that can borrow sufficient working funds on an unsecured basis directly from banks or other financial institutions. Furthermore, the fact that the accounts receivable are guaranteed by the factor usually strengthens the borrowing position of the client.

Maturity factoring with an assignment of equity. A facet of factoring that has become more prevalent in recent years is maturity factoring with an assignment of equity. As the diversification of industry continues to grow at an ever increasing pace, the needs of manufacturers, distributors, and processors for funds become greater and, to a certain extent, more competitive. Since standard methods for acquiring funds, however well they may have served in the past, may no longer be adequate, the institutions that supply funds to industry have had to evolve new plans and arrangements to meet the financial needs of their clients effectively. To accomplish these objectives, banks and factoring companies have cooperated to service mutual clients.

Maturity factoring with an assignment of equity is a first-rate example of these new developments. Essentially, this type of plan is a combination of conventional factoring and maturity factoring. The client that needs this type of factoring is one that wishes to borrow from a bank at banking rates, but that also requires additional funds in excess of its normal unsecured bank line. To satisfy this client, the factor now calls into play one of its best assets —flexibility of service.

By special agreement, the client assigns to the bank its equity in the credit balances with its factor. The factor agrees to remit the client's matured funds directly to the bank on the maturity dates. The client takes no advances against accounts receivable, but borrows needed funds directly from the bank. In actuality, the bank is advancing monies against the balances held by the factor for future payment. The accumulated funds that the factor pays to the bank are credited by the bank against the client's loan balance. This type of factoring permits the client to maintain its regular banking relationship and still borrow funds in amounts greater than it would be able to obtain on an unsecured note basis.

The assignment-of-equity technique is also particularly well suited to the solution of problems that occur between a manufacturer, processor, or distributor and its principal supplier. In certain cases a company may purchase all or most of its inventory from one source, creating a situation in which the supplier is forced to provide a credit line that may be disproportionate to the capital structure of the customer. Of course, it is to the mutual advantage of both to maintain the greatest possible flow of goods from supplier to customer, but the demands of credit prudence cannot be ignored. The factor's ability to tailor a plan to fit specific needs can provide a solution. The case history that follows illustrates this point.

A supplier of specialized equipment had a credit problem with a large-volume distributor of its product. The distributor had been doing an outstanding marketing job with the supplier's product. In fact, the supplier's sales department would have liked to double the distributor's inventory, thereby increasing both sales and profits substantially. However, the distributor already owed the supplier more than $100,000, an amount which exceeded the distributor's capital. The credit committee of the supplying company refused to increase the line of credit. An investigation by the factor disclosed that:

- The supplying company was virtually the sole supplier to the distributor.
- Although the distributor's operation was profitable, the bank would not increase its line of credit. This meant that the distributor did not have additional funds with which to prepay the supplier's invoices and, without prepayment, could not obtain additional shipments from the supplier.

Actually, the distributor was on a COD basis with regard to shipments above the credit limit. Yet one thing it did not have was cash, since its money was tied up in outstanding accounts receivable. From the supplier's credit standpoint, this seemed to be the only correct way to operate, but in the framework of marketing, the situation was creating a vacuum that competition was sure to fill.

. From the facts developed during numerous discussions, the factor designed a three-cornered arrangement. First, the distributor signed a factoring contract under which the factor agreed to purchase all the distributor's sales invoices. In addition, the distributor authorized the net proceeds of sales invoices assigned to the factor to be paid only to the supplier. As part of the arrangement, the supplier authorized the factor to advance to the distributor up to 20 percent of current sales received by the factor. This 20 percent withdrawal represented the distributor's markup over cost of the material sold, and permitted the seller access to funds to meet operating costs. The undrawn balance was to be paid directly to the supplier on monthly maturity dates against the supplier's invoices approved by the distributor.

This arrangement protected the supplier, since the proceeds of all sales of its product made by the distributor would be repaid by the factor. By acting as trustee for the supplier's funds, the factor was also protecting both parties from any losses due to bad debts.

Maturity factoring with an assignment of equity is also called participation factoring. The emergence of participation factoring as an important financing method stems primarily from one basic advantage: the borrower's ability to obtain a higher line of credit from his bank than would ordinarily be possible. This is because the factor guarantees the solvency of all the customers represented by the accounts receivable that it has purchased. Here are the salient features of the participation plan:

1. The borrower sells all of his accounts receivable,

and all new receivables as created, to the factor on a nonrecourse maturity basis.

2. At the outset, the borrower assigns to the bank a continuing right to the proceeds of his accounts receivable; that is, the credit balance at the factor.

3. The borrower then borrows whatever amount he needs directly from the bank at banking rates. The loan is secured by an assignment to the bank of the undrawn proceeds to be paid by the factor on specified due dates in the future.

4. Each month, the factor sends to the bank a statement of the borrower's account, showing the total sales factored during the previous month and the average due date of the invoices.

5. On the specified average due dates, the factor sends its check for the matured balances directly to the bank. The bank then applies the proceeds as a reduction of the loan.

6. The borrower obtains from the factor the services of credit protection, bookkeeping, and collection, for which he pays the factor a commission of about 1 to 1.5 percent of sales.

For example: A company may be able to obtain an $800,000 credit line on an unsecured basis from a bank at 8 percent interest. Under the new participation factoring plan, the company could sell the factor its accounts receivable and then assign its right to the proceeds from the factor as security to the bank for a loan at 8 percent interest. This raises the company's total potential line of credit from $800,000 to whatever level of accounts receivable the business can generate, which in most situations would be double or triple the $800,000 unsecured limit.

Bank participations also offer finance companies an

ideal method by which they may handle increased business and, at the same time, enjoy the advantages of spread risks, diversification, improved yield, and collaboration with specialists. The bank, too, benefits from participations. Occasionally, a bank is faced with one or more of the following circumstances: a period of tight money, necessary limitation of a customer's credit, or a restriction of an account because of bank capital limitations. By participating with a finance company in loans to qualified customers, the bank retains the account, enjoys a better than normal bank rate, and has a loan on a secured basis without the expense of policing the collateral. The borrower benefits from a finance company/bank participation by getting an interest rate somewhere between that of a bank and that of a finance company, while at the same time maintaining a relationship with his bank even though the loan is administered by the finance company.

It is apparent from the foregoing that the banks and factoring companies are rarely in competition. The company seeking short-term funds on the simplest, most economical terms should utilize the commercial bank—provided that its working capital will support the loan. However, if the client is seeking a combination of funds and specialized professional services, then his choice should be the factor.

The Commercial Finance Division

Collateral loans are the basic concern of the commercial finance division of the factor/finance company. It is able to offer its client larger sums of money with more flexible criteria than could be obtained from commercial banks. Loans are offered against varying types of collateral: accounts receivable, inventory, or equipment, as well as a combination of the assets available in each of these categories.

The client assigns all his accounts receivable to the finance company, which advances funds in a predetermined percentage against the accounts assigned. There is no notification to customers, and the finance company assumes no responsibility for credit risk or collection of outstanding receivables. Payment is made in normal fashion from the customer to the seller. The seller simply turns over the customer's payment to the finance division, which credits these funds toward his loan.

History. The commercial finance industry came into being in the early 1900's as an outgrowth of the old-line factoring that had started over one hundred years before. Early in the twentieth century, the introduction of new industrial equipment reduced the working capital of businesses below the traditional standards of commercial banks and forced these businesses to seek the services of the more adventuresome pioneers of the finance company. Contributing to further expansion of secondary financing were the needs created by the depression following the 1929 crash, the recognition afforded the finance industry during World War II by the federal Assignment of Claims Act of 1940, and the postwar expansion in business caused by increased consumer demand for goods.

It is estimated that in 1968 the finance company industry, including factors and commercial and consumer finance companies, was composed of over ten thousand companies with a total business volume in excess of $26 billion. The list of the "One Hundred" largest specialized finance companies, published by *American Banker* (May 19, 1969), showed combined capital funds as of December 31, 1969, of approximately $9.3 billion, and the volume of receivables purchased in 1968 of approximately $40.2 billion. Among such financial institutions as commercial banks, savings and loan associations, investment bankers, life insurance companies, charitable, educational and pension trusts, commercial paper houses, and various governmental agencies, only finance companies are specially equipped to handle the financial needs of small- and medium-size businesses in the process of development. Finance companies, not subject to the same degree of governmental regulation as other financial institutions, have greater flexibility in the conduct of their affairs. The greater administrative cost of handling secured loans is offset by interest charges at a level that assures the finance company an adequate profit after the cost of funds. The National Commercial Finance Conference, an association of most of the large- and medium-size factors and finance companies in the United States, has done much to support legislation that has liberalized the laws governing financial transactions, and has thus permitted its members to offer the greatest flexibility of financing services to American industry.

Accounts receivable financing. While in some respects similar to old-line factoring, commercial receivable financing differs in that the arrangement is always with recourse and usually is on a nonnotification basis. This arrangement overcomes the client's objection to old-line factoring's notification feature, and is more suitable where customer credit risk is unimportant to the client. The cost of this type of financing ranges from 11 to 20 percent per annum of daily average borrowed funds and is usually quoted as a fractional daily percentage. The cost can be higher or lower than old-line factoring, depending on the ratio of loans and volume which is usually determined by the average turnover in days of the accounts receivable.

Evaluation criteria. Contrary to some popular misconceptions, finance companies are not "graveyards for dying businesses." The typical client would probably fall into one of three general categories: new companies without a track record, rapid-growth companies overtrading on their capital, or borrowers who have suffered temporary reverses and cannot obtain financing from a bank.

The difference between the bank's and factor's approach to a typical situation lies in the criteria used to determine the amount of credit to be extended. Banks traditionally apply the usual accounting ratios, placing great emphasis on the capital structure in relation to the amount of credit to be granted. Finance companies, while also interested in capitalization, place their basic emphasis on the quality of the collateral to be pledged and on their ability to police this collateral and realize sufficient money to repay the loans in the event of liquidation. Inasmuch as they are relying on their ability to police the collateral, great demands are made on the knowledge of the finance company's personnel. Consequently, the finance company executive must have a broad knowledge of various industries and devote considerable time on a week-to-week basis studying the problems of each borrower.

When processing a new account, the finance executive first meets with the prospective borrower, examines and evaluates recent financial statements, and determines such things as the funds needed by the borrower to operate, the expected collateral coverage, the background of the individuals, and the history of the business. After the preliminary discussions and negotiations, which can take one meeting or several, the finance executive arranges for a member of his auditing staff to visit the premises of the prospect in order to prepare a survey of the records for a more detailed appraisal. Such a survey can take from one to several days and encompasses almost every aspect of the finances and operating procedures of the borrower. Special emphasis, of course, is placed on any peculiar aspects of the industry with regard to returns and discounts, advertising allowances, or other matters that might affect the collectibility of the accounts receivable. In determining the advance percentage to be made against the receivables, and the rate to be charged, a qualitative analysis is made of such things as bad debts, collection turnover days, customer delinquency percentages, items subject to customer offset, and the credit strength of large customers.

Next, a study of the paperwork procedures is undertaken to ensure the availability of such necessary data as invoice copies, receipts, customers' monthly statements, and monthly agings of accounts receivable. Finally, every account in the general ledger is examined so that any unusual transactions may be brought to light and discussed.

Legal aspects of closing. Under the Uniform Commercial Code, which is now in effect in every state except Louisiana, specific forms must be filed with the state or county recorder, or both, vetting for the collateral pledged by the borrower under specific security agreements. Whether the anticipated financing is to involve a straight receivable loan or the combination of receivables, inventory, chattel mortgages, and so on, it is necessary that a search of the state and/or county records be made to determine what prior filings are recorded. In addition, consideration must be given to the usury laws in the various states, as well as to the right-to-do-business laws of some states, particularly where the collateral pledged is inventory or equipment that is physically located in a foreign state.

A typical accounts receivable finance agreement is shown in the Appendix. Other forms generally used include corporate resolutions, personal and corporate guarantees, and subordinations, as well as cross-collateral, inventory, chattel mortgage, and letter of credit agreements. All these agreements, of course, provide maximum protection for the lender, since the main purpose of such agreements is not only to protect against third parties but to give the lender, in his dealings with the borrower, the greatest latitude in which to exercise his judgment. Because these agreements do have the effect of putting the borrower at a disadvantage, in that he can seldom hold the lender to any fixed obligation to lend money, the borrower should choose his lender with care, placing special emphasis on integrity and experience.

Operating the account. In its day-to-day relationship with the borrower, the commercial finance division deals with assignments of sales, turnover of collections, and requests for advances of funds. It must therefore review the sales assignments on a daily basis to determine their authenticity and collectibility. For example, a careful scrutiny of the checks received from customers may reveal differences in invoice dates, which may, in turn, be an indication of prefilling; in the event of a skipped or on-account payment, the invoices involved are questioned. Since significant changes involving collection turnover days, the amount of credits issued, and customer delinquency percentages may be an indication of a serious business condition, great emphasis is placed on learning the individual patterns of various accounts.

Once a month, the receivable agings and customers' statements are reviewed to determine the delinquency percentage and provide data for the revolving verification program. Verification of all accounts (usually to the extent of about 10 percent of the outstanding each month) is part of the constant effort to limit the risk of accounts receivable financing fraud. Periodic surprise audits of the borrower's books are conducted on a revolving basis, every 60 or 90 days; this service includes a study of the cash receipts and disbursements, a reconciliation of the accounts receivable with the finance company records, an aging of the accounts payable to be certain that clients' bills are kept under control, a determination that tax payments are current, and an estimate of the general progress of the business. Wherever inventory or chattel mortgage loans are involved, an examination of these assets is also performed. Internally, the finance company keeps records of the status of all insurance policies covering assets pledged.

Liquidation procedures. While few lenders would make a loan in expectation of a liquidation or bankruptcy arrangement, every loan should be controlled in such a way that the lender can collect on the collateral independently. Because accounts receivable financing does not involve notification to the buyer, sufficient information, including statements showing the exact amount owing, must be available at all times, so that the finance division can notify all the account debtors (on the client's letterhead) of the assignment by the client. In the event of client insolvency, it would also be necessary to notify the postal authorities to forward all mail to the finance company. Postal offices also require an authorization on the client's letterhead. Where the collateral is inventory or equipment, more legal expense is involved in first gaining physical possession of the assets. Furthermore, care must be exercised in conducting sales of the assets according to legal requirements.

In any bankruptcy proceeding, a creditors committee or a trustee will immediately look into the nature of all the transactions with the secured lender, and, in the event that the proper documentation has not been made, or in the event that preference can be proved, will attempt to set aside the rights to collateral. Accordingly, a good working knowledge of the bankruptcy laws is necessary in order to avoid errors that might cost the lender his collateral.

Other services. The commercial finance division also lends funds through the technique of chattel mortgages on income-producing equipment, and makes percentage advances against the value of pledged or warehoused inventory. Loans in these categories are usually made in conjunction with an accounts receivable financing arrangement as part of a total finance package.

In certain seasonal industries, a company may have to build inventory in the early part of the year in order to be able to ship heavily at a later date. In the early part of the year, therefore, receivables are low and cash availability limited. Since the inventory level is quite high in relation to sales during this period, the finance company may make a percentage loan against inventory to supplement the cash available on the receivables, thus providing the client with what could be considered a revolving loan against a fluid combination of assets.

The growing trend in American industry to lease or rent technologically advanced equipment rather than own it has opened up new and as yet unlimited market opportunities for financing. This trend has prompted many factoring companies to expand the scope of their commercial finance divisions to handle equipment leasing and also to finance equipment time sales for dealers selling income-producing equipment.

3

International Factoring

THE surge in international trade since the end of World War II has prompted many factoring companies to develop specialized services for foreign companies selling in the United States, either through American subsidiaries or through agents, as well as for domestic firms importing merchandise from abroad. These services are in reality an extension of the services offered by the old-line factoring houses to European manufacturers in the early 1800's.

The factoring arrangement itself is essentially the same as conventional factoring, providing for credit risk protection, accounts receivable bookkeeping, and customer collection. In addition, the factor provides letters of credit through commercial banks to its importing clients in favor of their foreign suppliers. When bills of lading representing a foreign shipment are received by the factor, he turns them over to his client in exchange for a trust receipt. At that time, the necessary funds for import duties and other charges must be paid, and are sometimes advanced by the factor. The accounts receivable created by ultimate shipment are turned over to the factor in repayment of the funds or credit initially advanced. The extent to which funds are advanced depends on the creditworthiness of the client.

Advantages of Import Factoring

The particular advantage of import factoring stems from the ability of the factor to obtain substantial letter of credit facilities from both domestic and foreign commercial banks. The factor's capital, much larger than that of the importer client, enables these banks to grant letters of credit in greater amounts than could be obtained by the client alone. Thus the factor's capital becomes the device through which the client is able to increase the volume of his imports and service a greater potential market.

A Typical Example

The following case history deals with a company whose sales and profits were significantly affected by this technique.

An importer and distributor of consumer electronic products, which started with relatively modest capital and a great deal of sales and merchandising talent, made a highly desirable contact with a major foreign producer of electrical and electronic products. The foreign manufacturer was highly impressed with the talent, imagination, and energy of the young company's management, and after a few years of association agreed to an exclusive relationship for the sale of its products in the United States. The manufacturer, a giant corporation, also devoted its research and development facilities to creating new designs and technical improvements in coordination with the American company. Finally, the foreign manufacturer further agreed to allow its products to be sold under the label of the American importer-distributor.

From 1962 to 1963, sales increased by 60 percent and profits by 500 percent. In 1964, sales doubled and profits increased by 30 percent. All these statistics justified the confidence shown by the foreign maufacturer, and naturally delighted the stockholders of the American firm. However, the picture was not as bright as this balance-sheet prosperity might have indicated, because there were still a number of hard-core problems.

Problem 1. The foreign manufacturer constantly pressed the distributor to increase its sales volume if the distributor wished to retain exclusive selling rights in the United States.

Problem 2. Whenever the manufacturer was ready to ship merchandise, the distributor was required to open a letter of credit in favor of the supplier prior to shipment. This, of course, required the American firm to utilize large cash and credit facilities to support its inventory, an inventory which was afloat for several weeks before landing, warehousing, and sorting for shipment against orders.

Problem 3. The rapid growth of sales required the maintenance of an inventory that was continually expanding, not only in volume, but also in diversification of models. As a result, the cash flow and working capital of the American firm were strained still more.

Problem 4. As volume grew, so did outstanding accounts receivable. The problem was magnified when large domestic competitors offered their own dealers and distributors long terms at certain seasons of the year as an inducement to take in large stocks of merchandise in advance of normal selling periods. Forced to remain competitive, the importer-distributor offered extended terms to its customers. Thus the double impact of a rapidly expanding volume and a lengthening accounts receivable collection period compounded the strain on an already tight cash flow.

Problem 5. When volume was relatively modest, the distributor sold essentially to well-rated customers, and the credit concentration per customer was small. However, as volume expanded, sales were made to less well-rated customers in order to broaden the market for the distributor's products. More models were also sold in greater depth to each individual customer. Coupled with the extension of longer selling terms, this tended to create larger and larger credit exposures per customer. With every dollar of working capital and profit sorely needed to finance its overly expanding inventory, the distributor could not afford any attrition of capital through bad debt losses.

Problem 6. From its inception, the American distributor had enjoyed a good relationship with a bank which was favorably impressed with the ability of management to enhance the sales of its products and to convert its growing volume into growing profits. But the financing of a growing and more complicated inventory created an ever increasing need for letter of credit facilities, while the burden of carrying an expanding dollar amount of accounts receivable called for more and more cash funds. Overhead and salaries had to be covered. Freight and duty payments had to be paid in cash whenever merchandise was received from abroad. Finally, the bank reluctantly notified the distributor that, on the basis of its capital structure, the company had reached the end of the bank's ability to accommodate its financing needs.

Management was now faced with what really amounted to a life or death decision for the firm. It could attempt to raise new capital (not readily available), or it could restrict the growth of the company until the profits earned would build a sufficient capital increase to support increased credit requirements.

The latter alternative had at least two major drawbacks. First, the distributor had spent a great deal of time, money, and effort to develop an efficient sales force and to create a demand for its products through a costly advertising program. But even more important was the very real possibility that the foreign manufacturer would change distributors because it felt that the current American distributor was financially unable to support a growing sales volume. Therefore, the distributor proceeded to attempt to raise new capital.

In this instance, the problems had been created by excessive activity. A factoring arrangement seemed to be the most practical solution to these problems.

Although the company had used up its letter of credit lines with its bank, this problem disappeared with the establishment of the factoring arrangement. Now, when the company had to open a letter of credit, the factor guaranteed the application to the bank, thus substituting its greater financial responsibility for the considerably smaller capital of the client; the bank was now willing to open letters of credit in almost unlimited amounts. And when the letters of credit were negotiated and converted into bankers' acceptances, the factor assumed the responsibility for paying the acceptances at maturity. Shipping documents were made to the account of the factor, which held a general lien and trust receipts covering the purchased goods from the time the bills of lading were released to the client until the goods were sold in the United States. At that time the factor acquired the ownership of the accounts receivable. This arrangement assured the availability of greatly increased inventory shipments.

When these shipments arrived in the United States, the factor advanced the funds to pay the freight bills and duties. The goods were then delivered to the company's warehouse and held there, subject to the factor's control, until shipped to customers against orders that had previously been approved by the factor's credit department.

When accounts receivable were created, they were purchased without recourse by the factor, which assumed the credit risk and the responsibility for collection. At the time of purchase, the factor credited 100 percent of the net amount to the account of the importing company as a repayment of the funds already advanced, and also as a deposit against the acceptances to be paid in the future.

During the first year of the factoring arrangement, the distributor expanded its sales by another 75 percent and its profits by 50 percent. The flexibility of financing offered by the factoring arrangement provided ample funds and facilities with which to maintain sufficient inventory levels to service customer needs; the credit protection offered by nonrecourse factoring assured the preservation of earned profits; and assumption of the accounts receivable bookkeeping and collection functions by the factor permitted the company to concentrate its attention on product design and sales.

A word of caution. Since import factoring requires a sophistication and knowledge of the intricacies of importing problems, as well as a familiarity with foreign document procedures and the performance habits of supplying countries, a client should investigate carefully his prospective factor's experience in this area before signing a factoring agreement.

Other Factoring Arrangements

The factoring plans described to this point have one thing in common: Funds are obtained by the client against accounts receivable only after the merchandise has been shipped to the customer. What of the client whose cash needs predate that moment when its products leave its factory or warehouse?

Loans or advances can be provided by the factor in the form of short-term preseasonal loans for inventory buildup on a secured or an unsecured basis, depending upon such matters as the length of time for which the funds are required and the proportion of the loan to the client's capital. Also, in conjunction with regular factoring arrangements, chattel mortgages can be taken against collateral of plant and equipment, and can be repaid over a term period rather than on a seasonal basis.

Export Factoring

A recent development in the factoring industry is the growth of export or overseas factoring. Prompted by the growth of American companies in overseas trade, the increased popularity of selling merchandise on open account instead of by letter of credit, the need for capital abroad, and the export insurance program started by the Kennedy administration in 1961, the American factor has gone abroad.

The volume of overseas factoring in 1966—both domestic and international—was estimated at about $450 million. Volume appears to be growing by 25 percent annually and should continue at that rate for perhaps another five years, at which point there could be some degree of market saturation. In overseas factoring, the American factor must compete not only with other American factors but, in recent years, with locally owned factors which do only a domestic business in the industrial nations of Europe and Asia.

There are some basic problems with regard to export factoring that have not yet been completely solved. It is difficult, for example, to obtain credit information on overseas customers, and even more difficult to collect from them. Some American factors have established overseas offices to handle credit approvals and collections, but an office merely for collection purposes is simply not equipped to compete for the large share of international trade that is done on open account, where the seller merely bills the customer, who promises to pay by a certain date.

Overseas Operations

Realizing the need to be intimately familiar with the business and financial traditions of the nations in which they intend to operate, American factors have initiated partnerships or cooperative arrangements with local factors or banking interests.

One of the first factoring companies to venture overseas set up a Swiss holding company and then established factors in 12 European countries. The Swiss partner owns 50 percent of each company, while local banking interests own the balance. This factoring group indicates that the largest segment of its volume is in traditional nonrecourse factoring, and that, at this stage, domestic factoring accounts for a far larger volume than does international. However, some of the companies are inclined to believe that the international sector of their business may eventually become greater than the domestic.

Another major American factor took a more indirect route into the European market. It first undertook to build up its import factoring business and, after a year, began a similar drive for export factoring. Its first operation in Europe was really a test run, with no partnership or cooperative arrangement. When the accumulated knowledge and experience from this initial venture were put to work in a second European country, the factor entered into a partnership with local banking interests. At the present time, the factor plans to expand into a number of other countries in Europe, Africa, and South America.

This factoring house believes that, if it is to do a really meaningful job, it must provide its clients with a full line of industrial financing. In its setup, factoring is offered as part of a broader program that also includes the potentially more profitable area of commercial financing.

Service fees are generally a bit higher overseas than they are in the United States. When money is advanced against receivables, it is usually in local currency, and the cost depends on local borrowing rates. The type of factoring may also be influenced by the tax structures of the various countries. In Germany, for instance, where there are tax advantages for a manufacturer in recourse factoring, only a very few cases involve advances against receivables on a nonrecourse basis.

It appears likely that most American companies seeking to enter the overseas factoring market will take the route of cooperative arrangements or partnerships. In the cooperative arrangement, the American factor handles the sales of the foreign factor's clients here in the United States. Conversely, the foreign factor handles the sales of the American factor's clients in its own country. This type of arrangement can overcome one of the major drawbacks in international factoring—that is, the difficulty of finding trained personnel overseas. For those factoring houses that favor the partnership arrangement, the problem boils down to finding the right partner. The officers and operating specialists of one American factor spent six months indoctrinating, training, and providing systems and procedural background to personnel and management of an English factoring company, which at this writing has completed approximately four years of operation in the British Isles. The export of ideas and operational knowledge is in some degree a measure of the vitality and validity of this homegrown product.

Future Expansion

The entrance of American factoring into Europe is still so recent that definitive lines of action have not yet been established. One of the firms now doing business in Europe thinks that the high cost of initial entry may prevent an invasion of the continent by American factors, but, regardless of cost, an increasing number of American factors are doing business in Europe or are in the process of making arrangements to do business in Europe.

As American business expands overseas, it wants its overseas operations to be handled as extensively and as efficiently as those in the domestic sector. The American factor that is not established overseas or is uncertain about an overseas venture is simply giving away business to those American firms already on the scene.

Throughout its long history, the factoring industry has always been alert to changes in the economy and quick to adjust to these changes, evolving modifications of old techniques or developing new ones to offer effective tools to the management of American business. This flexibility and adaptability will enable the factoring industry to continue to serve the financial needs of American industry as it broadens its position throughout the world.

4

The Factor
and the Commercial Bank

THE factor/finance company is not in general competition with the commercial bank. On the contrary, it uses substantial amounts of bank funds to service the money requirements of its own clients. It seems highly unlikely that commercial banks would supply funds to factoring companies in order to stimulate competition; there is more than enough rivalry among the commercial banks themselves to assure that the needs of qualified banking customers are served. Actually, a broad financial area exists within which the two financial institutions can and do cooperate to solve the money problems of mutual clients.

The Larger Bank

We are in an era of mergers unprecedented in the history of American business, and the banking industry has not been immune to this trend. As fewer and fewer banks remain on the business scene, the surviving institutions have at their disposal enormous resources that put them in a better position to compete aggressively for a larger share of the financial market.

The salesman's byword that the amount of sales is in direct proportion to the number of calls made has not been lost on the banking industry. Branches are being built as rapidly as possible to make it convenient for both the consumer and industry to conduct business with the bank. So today, on the corner that once housed the small independent bank, with its bank officers who knew all the small businessmen in the area, stands the branch of a giant institution.

This trend to larger banking amalgams affects the way the bank conducts its business. The modern multiservice bank handles an astonishing variety of complex operations —national and international, corporate and personal, civic and commercial. Credit cards, payroll services, trust activities, and merger and acquisition assistance are all handled with the aid of giant, sophisticated computers. This welter of specialized functions has fostered a need for efficient, specialized personnel. The modern loan officer sitting at the desk of a streamlined branch in a large city requires a familiarity with functions and procedures with which his counterpart in the old, independent bank had little involvement. His training has been intensive and varied; he is encouraged constantly to further his education and training so that he may be exposed to the many new developments in financial techniques that grow out of the ever expanding needs of both American and foreign economics.

The commercial bank deals with public deposits, and is increasingly subject to federal and state regulation, which acts to protect the financial integrity of the banking system. In a sense, the commercial banker is the trustee of public funds. His function is to lend these funds prudently to companies and individuals of demonstrated capacity to use the borrowed funds wisely and for profit. His long experience in dealing with strong customers has made him cautious about dealing with the untried newcomer or continuing his support of companies whose profit trend is negative. His prudence is justified, considering that his role, for the most part, is as a lender of unsecured funds.

Aware of the many and complex demands on their banking officers, and mindful of the need for a different specialization of background, the senior managements of those banks that have developed or acquired factoring operations have generally gone to the old-line factoring or commercial finance companies to staff these operations. Expansion of commercial banks into the factoring and commercial finance field has created a need for specialized personnel familiar with the flexible but specialized transactions and techniques utilized in these activities.

The Structure of the Finance Company

The attitudes, techniques, and point of view of the finance company executive must necessarily be somewhat different from those of the banker. He designs a financing package from a set of facts, from arrangements of assets and liabilities, and from his own and his company's wide background of experience and specialized knowledge. He is, in effect, an architect who creates a structure to solve a financial problem.

Since finance companies charge higher interest rates than do banks, they can afford to lend money on a basis that would be unprofitable for a bank. Protected by legal devices such as liens, chattel mortgages, bonded or field warehouses, and assignments of accounts receivable, the finance company loan officer administers the loan secured by the assets against which he is lending. Here again, we see the distinction between the bank and the finance company: the bank makes unsecured loans against a customer's capital strength while the finance company lends against assets that are pledged specifically for the purpose of the loan. Since this loan is a percentage of the appraised liquidation value of assets, the secured lender—that is, the finance company—can usually liquidate its position without loss even if the client should be unable to repay the borrowed funds. It is the security of the loan that gives the finance company the opportunity to be of service to industry with a much greater degree of flexibility than the commercial bank can afford. And it is the cost of policing the collateral as well as the higher cost of money that necessitates the higher cost of interest charges.

The Financial Service Team

Many companies factor their accounts receivable on a maturity basis and borrow their requirements on a note basis from commercial banks. In many cases, commercial banks will recommend factoring to borrowers when the loan is substantial and the borrower's accounts receivable involve high-risk exposure concentrations.

Several important elements that can be provided only by the factoring house form the basis for the bank's recommendation in such a case. Maturity factoring provides flexible credit risk insurance. Outstanding accounts receivable are guaranteed on a dollar-for-dollar basis. With the exact date established as to when the client will receive payments of matured receivables, the bank and the borrower can agree on convenient repayment schedules. A typical case history will serve to illustrate how the factor and the commercial bank work together in other ways to solve the financial problems of business.

A manufacturer of women's sweaters had anticipated an increase in demand for its product, and had prepared meticulously so that it would be able to exploit fully these new sales opportunities. The bank had extended a substantial line of credit so that this manufacturer could purchase large quantities of yarn and also step up production of finished goods inventory.

But for several reasons, including unseasonably warm fall weather, the anticipated surge in sales failed to develop. The manufacturer was under severe pressure to meet both its payroll and maturing yarn bill payments. The only way it could relieve the situation was to market a quantity of merchandise at a loss.

By the end of the fall season, the foreseeable results had indeed developed. The combined effects of lower sales volume and lack of gross profit had caused the manufacturer to sustain a large operating loss. Working capital was weakened. Already operating under the burden of an inventory of raw material in excess of normal requirements, the manufacturer was under further contractual obligation to absorb additional shipments of yarn into this swollen inventory. Yet, if the company was to continue to operate during the coming months, it needed additional borrowed funds to support its inventory and to meet payrolls. It could not obtain these additional funds from the lending bank, which had expected the loan to be liquidated in the normal course of business sometime near the end of the calendar year. Indeed, the bank still wanted payment, despite the fact that loss of working capital and the pressing need for a large amount of cash made it impossible for the manufacturer to repay the loan at this time.

This was the problem that the bank loan officer asked the factor to help solve, both for the bank and for its manufacturer customer. Highly specialized auditors of the factor's commercial finance division were sent to the manufacturer's premises to conduct a detailed examination of its operations. The inventory and future commitments were examined, and cash flows and budgets prepared that indicated the peaks and valleys of future cash needs. A thorough analysis of the data compiled by the auditors enabled the factor to develop a sound financial plan. To solve the manufacturer's most pressing problem—the need for large amounts of cash—this plan called for the factoring company to lend the manufacturer 80 percent of the value of its current accounts receivable as well as approximately 50 percent of the cost value of its raw yarn inventory. A field warehouse was established in the manufacturer's plant to control yarn inventory, a procedure that would be required for about six months. After receiving an assignment of the existing accounts receivable, the factor advanced the necessary funds to repay the bank loan and provided cash to meet payrolls and maturing accounts payable.

Thus the bank received repayment of its loan, and suppliers' bills were met on time. Not only was the manufacturer able to remain in business and operate profitably during the following year, but at the end of 16 months its net worth had grown to a point where it was greater than it had been prior to the time that it had suffered its loss.

Why had the factor/finance company been able to find a solution to this manufacturer's problem while the commercial bank could not? The criteria by which the commercial finance company judges a prospective client's financial competence are somewhat different from those of a bank. Although the client's balance sheet is an important consideration, the commercial finance company places less emphasis on the size of capital equity than does the commercial bank, and more emphasis on the strength of pledged collateral and the borrower's potential ability to market his product successfully. Realistic and accurate conclusions on both of these issues require intimate knowledge of the borrower's industry.

In the case of this manufacturer, records showed that it had operated profitably in the past; that it had a history of competence and integrity; and that it had assets which, when pledged to the factor, would provide adequate security for the loan. Furthermore, studies indicated that the manufacturer required only a reasonable sales volume in order to generate profits, and that careful inventory controls would produce an orderly reduction of inventory excesses within a short period of time. Shrinking of inventory would be accompanied by a growth in the accounts receivable level, permitting repayment of the inventory loan and the removal of the field warehouse arrangement after the six-month period. The financial plan developed for the sweater manufacturer was based on all these elements. Such tailor-made financial arrangements are not unusual.

Bank Participations

However, there are situations in which the commercial bank may wish to retain a lending relationship with the customer, but wants to lessen the amount of funds it is lending as well as limit the risk. The bank may turn over the administration of the loan to the specialist in secured lending, the factor/finance company. The finance company lends in its normal fashion—against accounts receivable, on a nonnotification basis, with recourse to the seller—and sells an interest in the loan to the commercial bank. The relationship is with the finance company, which lends all the money, but the rate is reduced by floating the bank's participation at a lower rate. Both institutions share the risk, and the customer gets the advantage of frequent audits and counseling advice that the commercial finance company supplies as a regular feature of its loan.

At times, a commercial bank may be dealing with a customer whose rate of growth creates a need for funds that exceeds the bank's legal lending limit. The bank may be reluctant to invite a larger bank to participate in the loan on the theory that it may ultimately lose the customer to its larger competitor. Instead, the bank often asks a commercial finance company to participate in the loan, so that the lending bank in no way jeopardizes its lending relationship with the particular customer.

Participation loans are not unique, but a survey of 2,000 commercial banks conducted in 1963 revealed that over 75 percent of these banks had never participated in loans with a commercial finance company. Now an increasing number of banks are investigating or engaging in participation loans. Participation loans extend one step further the ability of the banks (in conjunction with factoring companies) to increase their loans to young firms or growth companies. Participation loans permit banks to overcome the pinch of tight money conditions and to extend loans beyond either the limits of the credit of the borrowing company or the restrictions imposed on the bank by its own capital limitations.

For the growth company, there are certain real advantages to borrowing jointly from a bank and a finance company. The principal one, of course, is that the company can obtain the amount of working capital that it needs, or at the very least, a much greater amount than could be obtained from a bank alone. The borrower generally pays a lower interest rate than he would if the money were supplied entirely by the finance company.

Furthermore, the borrower receives, at no cost, certain services and information from the finance company. All assigned accounts are verified on a regular monthly basis, or more often, if circumstances so dictate. All receipts accompanying the borrower's invoices are carefully scrutinized and occasionally checked with the delivery company or railroad. Such problems as skipped bills, overdue items, and discrepancies are noted and investigated. The credit of the borrower's customers is continuously reviewed. Studies and analyses are made of any concentration of shipments to a single customer. Accounts receivable are aged at least once a month. Delinquent accounts are investigated to find the reason for nonpayment. Trends of the borrower's sales, gross profits, turnover of receivables, ratios of sales to inventory, and so on are plotted and observed.

There is no doubt that these services are instituted by the finance company for its own protection. Nevertheless, the borrower also derives benefit from them. The men who are guiding and advising the borrower are experts in business management, and therefore help contribute to the success of the borrower's business.

Case Studies

An imposing number of companies have utilized the. services of commercial finance or factoring organizations to assist their growth to a point where they eventually qualify for public ownership and more conventional forms of financing. Each year the National Commercial Finance Conference, Inc., at its annual convention honors the chief executives of these companies by presenting "awards for achievement in business growth, made possible through use of commercial finance company funds." In addition to paying tribute to these companies, the event is an affirmation of the value of secured lending—of the vital role of finance companies in helping to build our industries. The roster of these companies includes such outstanding names as United Artists Corporation, National Airlines, Monsanto Chemical Company, Diner's Club, Helene Curtis, Dow Chemical Company, Buitoni Foods, and Mattel, Inc. (Barbie Dolls). Let's look at the histories of some of these companies.

United Artists Corporation. In the late 1940's, when the entire film industry was at the brink of decline, United Artists Corporation was in dire financial straits. Founded in 1919, the company showed a net loss of $517,000 in 1948, $209,000 in 1949, and $871,000 in 1950. Debt-ridden, it seemed ready to fall into bankruptcy. Then, in 1951, a new management team took over and turned to a commercial finance company to finance the revival of the company.

In March 1951, the company received a first advance of $3.5 million from the commercial finance company, secured by receivables and other assets. With the commercial finance company's funds, United Artists contracted for all the available films it could buy. This permitted it to guarantee its exhibitors enough top-quality films for a year. The exhibition contracts which resulted were assigned to the finance company. On the security of these contracts, the finance company was able to supply funds by which United Artists financed rapid expansion of its activities. By the end of 1951, the first year of the corporation's association with the commercial finance company, United Artists was able to show a profit of $313,000. And by 1957, United Artists had built its worldwide gross revenues to more than $70 million.

Helene Curtis Industries, Inc. Helene Curtis was established in Chicago in 1927 to manufacture facial mud packs. By 1932 sales had been built to $373,000, although net worth was still relatively small ($34,000). Financing was needed to exploit the vast potential market for Helene Curtis beauty products, but in 1932 there was a dearth of lenders and investors. Finally, the company was able to secure financing from a commercial finance company, which provided funds against the pledge of time-payment mortgage and conditional sales contracts made with beauty shops. In 1932 the company pledged only $20,000 in notes and accounts receivable. By the outbreak of World War II, annual sales had risen to $3 million, and by 1946 the company's sales volume had reached $14.3 million, helped in part by defense contracts to produce needed military equipment.

The end of the war brought a period of harsh readjustment. Defense contracts had expired and the competition in the beauty care field had caught up to Helene Curtis. The company undertook a period of intensive product development, and by 1949 sales had climbed back to $8.2 million. At the end of that year, the relationship with the commercial finance company had grown from the $20,000 in pledges in 1932 to a direct obligation to the finance company of $1.2 million. Early in 1950 the company became eligible for a term loan from one of the major insurance companies and the finance company's advances were repaid during that year.

Mattel, Inc. In June 1954, Mattel, Inc., had net sales of $4.9 million, net income of $86,500, and net worth of $683,597. At that time the company began to factor its receivables. The original factoring funds paid off a short-term bank loan secured by accounts receivable. In addition, extra advances during the peak season enabled the company to produce inventory earlier, thereby leveling the production activity throughout the year. In the years until the finance company relationship was terminated (December 31, 1958), Mattel spent an enormous amount on research and development. The Barbie doll was developed during that period and was introduced just after termination with the finance company.

Meanwhile, Mattel, Inc., had undergone rapid growth both in sales and profits. Net sales for the year 1958 were $13.9 million and net income $695,136, while net worth was approximately 2½ times greater than it had been in 1954. Today Mattel, Inc., is the largest toy manufacturer in the United States.

5

The Client-Factor Relationship

Now that we have established the various services of the modern factoring company, it would be worthwhile also to understand the type of business relationship that the factor maintains with its client. Many a businessman in a factoring relationship regards the factor much as he regards his accountant or lawyer: as a professional adviser to assist in the formulation of business policy.

The Factor as a Business Counselor

The wide exposure to the operation of many types of business enables the factoring executive to develop a working knowledge of markets, production developments, distribution techniques, and corporate financial planning. Here are brief examples of how this knowledge can be used to benefit a client.

Example 1. A manufacturing client informs a factoring executive that he is considering expanding his production. He is uncertain whether to build a new plant or to find outside facilities to handle his production on a contract basis. The problem is not simple, since the client will need additional production only during certain periods. The executive who handles this client's affairs contacts another of his clients who has a plant approximately 50 miles distant from the first client. The second client's plant is currently underemployed during the period in which the first client needs additional production, and has had experience manufacturing the first client's basic product. A phone call confirms the availability of the needed production, and the first client is soon delivering merchandise to his customers from an up-to-date, efficient factory without a costly investment in fixed assets.

The first client has been spared the need for tying up working capital in new fixed assets, and has avoided the high costs of setting up a new plant. The second client is also pleased, because he is able to run his plant at near capacity throughout the year, utilizing his investment more efficiently and maintaining a highly trained effective labor force on a year-round basis.

Example 2. A textile manufacturing client from New England discusses with the factor a new type of fabric that he is weaving at his mill. This fabric should add sales and profits to his operation and also improve his total manufacturing efficiency through greater plant utilization. However, his sales force has had little experience marketing this type of fabric. A factoring executive with extensive experience in the textile field is able to recommend a successful selling agent who has been looking for an additional mill to represent. This connection proves to be a mutually profitable union.

Example 3. About ten years ago, two principals of a modest sales representative company consulted a factor about launching their own toy manufacturing company. They had been doing a good job selling the products of other manufacturers, and, since they were familiar with all phases of the toy industry—product design, marketing, and sales—they felt that they could expand into manufacturing. They had just purchased a small toy company.

After discussing their plans and examining all the data thoroughly, the factor agreed to give their operation modest financial assistance, and, in a few years, assisted in the purchase of a second and then a third company. Soon after the three operating companies had been integrated into one, a fourth opportunity for expansion arose. The product line of acquisition number four was not competitive; in fact, the product actually rounded out the line and introduced a highly desirable contraseasonal aspect into the total sales picture.

The normal toy industry pattern is one of very light shipments through the first half of the year and heavy shipments concentrated in the period from August to December. The new acquisition's product, on the other hand, was shipped actively to stores and distributors during the first quarter of the year. In addition, the efficiency of consolidating some of the manufacturing of this product with the factory output of another division would result in an effective lowering of total manufacturing costs for the combined operation. And since the same selling organization would be handling distribution, product sales would be no problem.

As the young company continued to grow and prosper, it decided to increase its capital base in order to support even greater expansion. A portion of its stock was sold to the public, significantly increasing the company's paid-in capital. Within ten years of the company's formation, when it had begun with $300,000 in sales, it was shipping more than $30 million in diversified products and was earning substantial profits for its stockholders.

Over these ten years, the factor had been the prime source for funds to finance acquisitions and growth. Even after the company had gone public, it continued to call upon the factor for financial participation to provide extra cash flow for rapidly expanding production. Today, the factor's management is a member of the company's financial management committee, and acts as an adviser to the firm's board of directors.

Indeed, the president of the company has stated that the company will continue to use the services of the factor even if it does not need to borrow funds, since the costs of the factor's credit and collection services are more reasonable than the cost of providing these services internally. Furthermore, being freed from concern about credit risk, the company can concentrate on selling and production, and can farm out accounts receivable bookkeeping to a professional organization, obtaining sophisticated data processing reports and management advice.

Example 4. Here is an example of how the modern factoring organization can save a business from disintegration. For many years, one individual's acumen and wealth dominated a large segment of the textile greige goods business. The organization consisted of a selling organization that sold greige goods, manufactured by a group of four mills, directly to fabric converters. The mills were basically owned by the central company, although the manager of each mill had a financial interest in the mill that he was operating. The central organization also provided consolidated bookkeeping and billing facilities for all the mills, as well as a credit department to review and process orders received by the sales department. All yarn and raw materials for the mills were purchased through the central office, which then collected the accounts receivable for all sales made and debited the proceeds of each mill for payments made on its behalf to raw material suppliers.

However, the capital of the central organization basically belonged to one individual, and when he died, a major problem arose. The executors of his substantial estate, in the exercise of their responsibilities, decided that the estate should liquidate its textile holdings and invest the proceeds in government securities. From the standpoint of a conservative responsibility, no doubt, this was a correct decision. However, its result would be to dismantle an effectively operating business and to deprive many individuals of a source of livelihood.

Once again the resources of the factor were called upon. Examination revealed that all operating personnel wanted to stay with the business. The people in the selling and purchasing department wished to continue their relationship with the mills, and formed a separate corporation for this purpose. Each mill was separately incorporated to start with. In all but one case, the operating mill managers were able to bring in sufficient new capital for the mills to stand alone and obtain credit from yarn suppliers. In one instance, the factor took a mortgage on the mill and its equipment, and arranged a payout schedule geared to historical operating earnings. The effect of this loan was to provide a substantial working capital so that the mill would be able to obtain credit from yarn suppliers. After sales and cash flow analysis, the factor also agreed to lend temporary financing assistance through seasonal overadvances to each or all of the mills, as required.

Now only one problem was left. The executors, being prudent men, wanted the group to repay the estate for all the raw materials purchased before title to it was passed to each mill. This obligation ran to several million dollars, and the executors felt that they could not extend such credit to the new owners of the business. This development might have wrecked the new organization, but once again the factor was able to provide a solution. Cash flow and inventory turnover analyses showed that if the estate would wait 120 days for payment, this would be more than enough time for all the mills to process the yarn into piece goods to ship against customer's orders already on hand, thus creating accounts receivable credit balances with the factor before the date of payment. As a result of this study, the factor agreed to guarantee payment of the full value of the yarn inventory to the estate after 120 days, an arrangement which satisfied the executors concerned.

The arrangements were then consummated and, for the past nine years, the selling organization and the mills have been operating profitably. The factor, too, has enjoyed a substantial volume of business from a situation developed through initiative and long experience with a specific industry.

The Role of the Account Executive

The executives of the modern factor are called upon to deal with many firms, usually at top management level, in widely divergent industries. This enables them to develop insight and knowledge upon which to draw in counseling and advising their clients on business matters.

The account executive, so familiar in other areas of the business world, is present in the factoring company as well. It is the account executive who handles factor/client matters. He is usually an officer of his company, well versed in the business in which the client operates, and with sufficient authority to approve nonroutine requests by the client.

It is quite normal for a close relationship to develop between the client and his account executive. This in turn makes the client more willing to confide his business problems to the account executive, and to be more receptive to counseling on business matters, marketing, and other advisory services. As in most companies selling what is essentially a service, it is the quality of the relationship between the account executive and the client that creates the character of the factoring company in the marketplace.

The Personality of the Factoring Company

To a large degree, the character or personality of a factoring company will influence the prospective client in his selection of a factor. Just as the manufacturer seeks out the advertising agency that can meet as closely as possible his marketing needs, so the manufacturer choosing a factor will select the company that can most effectively solve his servicing and financing needs. This is an extremely important point to consider, for the very pronounced trend toward merger current in American industry is also very much in evidence in the factoring industry. We now have the phenomenon of very large and very small factoring companies, with little middle ground left.

One specific advantage of the large factoring house is that it has a wider range of capital and personnel resources to offer its client. However, there are also some definite disadvantages which the prospective client should weigh carefully. In many cases, the account executive's ready availability and authoritative flexibility are replaced by the slower-moving process of committee decision making. And, as happens so often in a large service company, the smaller client tends to become lost in the shuffle; the large client, by nature of the size of his business, has first call on the services of the more mature account executives.

The owner of a textile-converting business doing an annual volume of approximately $1.5 million recently signed a contract with a factoring company. When asked why he had picked that particular factor, he stated that the basis of his choice was that the factor was the largest in the country. Size had been the sole determinant. But the real criterion should have been the degree and type of service that the factor offered his particular business. He might have been wiser to select one of the medium-size or smaller first-line companies, where his volume would have been more signficant and where his company affairs would have received more personalized attention.

The Specialist

Just as there are commercial banks and savings banks, and advertising agencies for consumer accounts and for industrial accounts, so there are factoring houses which have become specialists in certain industries. This is a result of servicing a group of clients selling their products to the same group of customers. Here again, there are certain advantages and disadvantages of which the prospective client should be aware.

One of the more obvious advantages lies with the factor's credit department, which has a built-in reservoir of firsthand knowledge of the operations of the customers whose credit it is guaranteeing. It understands the customers' problems, because it has dealt with them over a

64

period of time. This depth of experience, enabling the factor's credit men to become more familiar with many important customers in the field, allows the factor to facilitate speedy credit approvals for its clients.

On the other hand, the disadvantages of dealing with the specialist factoring house are also considerable. The factor servicing a number of clients selling to the same trade builds up accounts receivable heavily concentrated in a particular group of customers. Many of this factor's clients may be selling to the same customer, who at some point must have a theoretical credit limit. It is conceivable that, when this point has been reached, the factor may have to ration the total credit line among its many clients selling to the same customer. This would tend to reduce the amount of credit availability per customer for the clients of this factor. On the other hand, the factor servicing fewer clients selling to the same customers may be able to assume a larger dollar risk for each of its clients, thus enabling the clients to do a larger volume of business in the particular industry.

A good rule to follow in selecting a factor is to choose a house that is familiar with the industry and has had experience with the customers that the prospective client sells, and to avoid the factor that already has so many clients in the same field that credit line conflicts could shrink sales opportunities.

The Factor's Credit Department

The credit department is the heart of the factoring company. In fact, a prospective client often selects one factoring company over another because of the reputation of its credit department. Because the ability of the credit department to distinguish between a good risk and a poor risk can have a lasting effect, not only upon the stability of the factor, but also on the growth of the client's business, the credit department must be familiar with the operations, problems, and special nature of many industries. This places a premium on the experienced, sophisticated, inquiring credit man—a specialized professional in a specialized industry.

The credit man. The credit man usually has had a background of college-level education oriented toward finance and accounting. He has worked as a collection man for a time and has developed some insight into the consequences of poor credit decisions. Then he has had a period of apprenticeship to an experienced man whom he serves as assistant and leg man. Finally, after a sufficient training period, he is assigned as a full-fledged credit man to handle the customers in one or more specific industries, and his decisions, flexibility, and constructive attitudes become vital parts of the image of the company for which he works.

The accumulation of data. The expert credit man will probe for and find the significant data that will enable him to reach a decision when he is in receipt of orders from a client's customer. Certain procedures are automatic. He obtains a Dun & Bradstreet or other credit agency report on the customer and then discusses the customer's financial status with an officer of the bank that carries the account. In the case of an out-of-town customer, he may send a letter to the customer's bank requesting information regarding their relationship.

With these preliminary details completed, the credit man searches for more specific facts. If the agency report does not contain a reasonably current financial statement, the credit man may make direct contact with the customer or the customer's accountant for this important information. If the agency report contains the latest financial statement, but a significant period of time has elapsed since its issuance, the credit man may make contact with the customer's accountant and request either a verbal or a written résumé of the most current trial balance on the operations of the customer. If the accumulated data still do not permit him to make a final decision, he will probably make an appointment and visit the customer to see at first hand the nature of the customer's management, controls, internal techniques, inventory, and product line, and to obtain any other insights that might be developed in a personal visit.

All the accumulated information, impressions, and collected data are carefully recorded in the customer's credit file. They provide the basis for the decision to accept the credit risk on the current order as well as reference material for future transactions with the same customer. The files of a well-organized factor contain reams of pertinent information about the financial and operational affairs of thousands of customers operating in the broad spectrum of American business.

A Typical Example

Frequently, and particularly in certain industries, it is important for the credit man to follow the affairs of his customers very closely. This is most important in the case where a client sells a large amount of merchandise to a customer whose working capital is not commensurate with the amount of credit that it requires.

Let us say that the factor's client is a mill that weaves a line of styled textiles used by manufacturers of women's dresses. The credit man knows that the dress industry is highly volatile, based on styling and fashion. A producer whose line happens to be "hot" may double his capital in one season. On the other hand, if he guesses wrong, at the very least he may suffer a substantial loss; at worst he may have put himself into bankruptcy.

The credit man knows the dress industry—knows that the industry abounds with optimists who are convinced that they will forever guess right. He also knows that it requires far less investment capital to organize a dress-manufacturing operation than to organize a business that requires a substantial quantity of productive machinery. As a consequence, the average investment of a typical dress manufacturer is relatively modest, compared with the investment required in many other industries. A well-managed dress-manufacturing operation cuts its patterns on its own premises, sends the cut piece goods to contractors for sewing, ships finished garments to department stores, and often receives payment from its customer before it has to pay the factor for the piece goods supplier. If all goes well, the dress man, because of his rapid turnover, can do a very large volume on a moderate capital. And if he is successful, the rewards are rich.

The risk of guessing. A particular fabric of the client's line has been shipped to a dress manufacturer, which has cut sample styles using this fabric. The dress manufacturer has guessed right. The dresses appeal to the buyers, and large-volume orders result. To cover itself, the manufacturer places large fabric orders for current and future deliveries. The orders are called into the factor's credit department by the mill and handed to the credit man.

Automatically, the credit man checks the information on file and contacts the accountant for the dress manufacturer. He learns that the manufacturer has a substantial amount of orders on hand, expenses are in line with the volume, and the manufacturer looks forward to a good fall season. So on behalf of the factor the credit man accepts the responsibility for the initial purchase commitments of the manufacturer.

Buyer demand for its dress line continues, so the following week the manufacturer reorders the fabric from the mill, which again submits the orders to its factor. These new orders bring the ante up quite high. Conventional terms for textiles sold to dress manufacturers are net 60 days. The credit man knows that the factor will not be paid for the first shipment before eight weeks have passed.

During this period, demand for the manufacturer's line may continue high and he may continue to reorder fabric from the mill to fill his orders. Therefore, it is entirely possible that during this period the manufacturer's credit requirement from the credit man may exceed the manufacturer's entire working capital. That could be a problem. Should the credit man set a reasonable line and tell the manufacturer that he cannot obtain any more of the client's fabric when the line is filled?

The credit man could take this easy way out and avoid any deeper responsibility. However, the client's sales volume has grown steadily year by year, and it is now one of the factor's best clients. The credit man, by his skillful handling of the account, has been highly instrumental in the growth of the client's sales. But he also has to consider his employer. His responsibility is to do a constructive credit job so that he can help his client's sales and its customer's profits, provided that both can be accomplished without exposing the factor to a potential loss.

A personal call. With the ground rules well defined, the credit man decides that a visit to the dress manufacturer's premises may be helpful in reaching a decision. He knows exactly what kind of information he will need in order to make an intelligent decision. At the manufacturer's place of business, he is an astute observer. What kind of man is the owner? Is he well organized? How much experience has he had in the dress business? What is his inventory-to-volume ratio? What about his personal habits? Does he gamble?

With all the facts in his notebook and in his head, the credit man now confers with the manufacturer. The manufacturer realizes that the credit man is the key to the mill's fabrics and that an ample supply of these fabrics is essential to his own success. He cooperates with the credit man, answering questions, showing financial and sales records.

The credit man's decision. The credit man must still consider some intangible but important facts. When will the manufacturer's styles cease to excite the interest of the buyers? He must take into account the possibility of strikes, production mishaps, and delivery delays. He must also determine whether the manufacturer's other suppliers will cooperate. Will its bank continue its support? From the maze of data that he has finally compiled, the credit man will arrive at a decision that takes into account the safety of the factor, the sales requirements of his client, and the customer's opportunity for financial success.

Competition and Cooperation

As in all industries today, competition for clients among established factoring companies is extremely keen. New business opportunities are kept top secret, and top management is wary of furnishing any information to competitors which might lose a contract with a potential client. It is most interesting, however, that the credit departments of keenly competing factors are highly cooperative with each other.

Professional credit men cooperate. They exchange information and divulge their research and hard-earned confidences to their opposite numbers in other factoring houses. The highly developed information system that permits them to walk the credit tightrope with finesse and sensitivity requires information input from a wide variety of sources. The information that one credit man shares with another at a competing factoring company may sometime bring him a warning, a significant fact that will help him avoid a substantial loss.

This policy of information exchange is so highly developed that many factoring credit departments send a representative to weekly, biweekly, or monthly discussion meetings held by the various industry groups. These meetings provide a clearing house for credit information. Indeed, it is hard to think of a counterpart in any other industry that matches this phenomenon of cooperation and information exchange.

Many credit men have pioneered in the struggle against commercial fraud, fighting for legislation to eliminate the professional thief from the commercial world. They have established auditing criteria for accountants servicing clients in the industries which they check, and have spent a great deal of time and energy working for cooperation between credit men like themselves and certified public accountants for the ultimate benefit of the customer.

It is no accident that when a businessman has a particular problem with which he desires assistance he frequently visits the credit man, for whom experience has taught him respect; he has learned to depend on the credit man for sound business advice.

6

The Factoring Contract

THE basic factoring contract is written to provide for the protection of the factor/finance company, much the same as a written lease provides for the protection of the landlord. In many clauses, provision is made to give the factor the "discretionary privilege" of modifying the original agreement. This usually occurs after a period of experience has indicated to the factor that the original premise upon which the agreement was written is not valid.

The Factor's Discretion

Since the factor is advancing funds against sales, it must have discretion with respect to advances in order to protect itself against unpredictable risks. At all times the client is required to maintain a credit balance with the factor commensurate with the volume and character of its outstanding receivables. The size of the credit balance retained depends upon the factor's experience with the client and the client's customer.

For instance, if the factor is dealing with a toy manufacturer, it knows that there is a seasonal peaking of receivables at Christmas. Experience has taught the factor that the return of defective goods from customers will usually not be felt until early January. If this particular client has had a history of larger than normal customer returns, the factor may feel that a normal 10 percent reserve will not be adequate to absorb the claims. At the end of the calendar year, for a period of 30 days a larger reserve may be required of the client. Again, a manufacturer of tape recorders selling a new model to a distributor may be required to maintain a higher credit balance during the period when these sets are under the manufacturer's service warranty. If the factor's client is a manufacturer of a product that runs a greater risk of being damaged or spoiled, the factor will hold a higher reserve than for goods which do not exhibit these tendencies.

The company signing a factoring contract must understand that the factor is insuring the seller against credit risk only. The factor does not insure the seller against disputes and claims of customers. The client must also realize that the contract gives the factor, at all times, the option to increase the percentage of reserve held as a credit balance. The financial strength of the seller weighs heavily in determining the adequacy of the reserve.

Commissions. In the case of a conventional factoring relationship, the selling terms dictate how much cash investment the factor has in the accounts receivable of a given client. The greater the time lapse between shipment of the product and date of payment, the more cash the factor has invested in the receivable; furthermore, the risk assumed by the factor is also carried for a longer period. Thus the rate of commission for a receivable outstanding over 90 days will be greater than for one of much shorter duration.

Termination. Contracts are generally in force for one year, and renew automatically from year to year unless the client requests termination by written notice 60 days prior to the anniversary date, although the factor may terminate at any time on 30-day notice. In event of termination, the factor can again exercise its "discretionary privilege," holding as a reserve an amount equal to the total amount of outstanding receivables at termination. Experience has shown that, in a liquidating situation, the last 20 percent of outstanding receivables might require a cash reserve equal to 100 percent of that amount. These outstanding receivables are usually old claims uncollectable for merchandise reasons, incomplete assortment, or various other reasons. They are unadjusted claims and are the most difficult to collect.

Personal guarantee. Assumption of personal liability by the officers of a closely held company is viewed as particularly important by the factor where ownership and management are synonymous. If there is a refusal to sign such an agreement, the factor will usually require a subsantial cash reserve, if it does enter into an agreement at all. The factor will almost always require a personal guarantee in the case where the client will take a loan in excess of its equity with the factor.

The Contract

The following section provides a summary of the areas usually covered in the contract between the factor and the client. A typical contract is illustrated in the Appendix.

Section one. In section one are included many of the essential terms of the agreement, an undertaking by the client to have only one factor, a present assignment of all present and future accounts, and a statement that the factor purchases and will purchase accounts acceptable to it. Naturally, the factor will not purchase accounts that it does not find creditworthy; if the account is not acceptable, then the risk will remain with the client, since there has been no actual purchase. This, of course, does not affect the present assignment of such future receivables.

The client warrants and represents that each account, at the time of the actual assignment of an existing account, will be a bona fide and existing obligation arising out of the sale of merchandise or the rendition of services by the client in the ordinary course of its business. Such a warranty by the client is a representation that all of the conditions on its part to be performed in the contract with its own customer have been performed, and protects the factor from several situations, for example, purchasing an invoice before the merchandise has been delivered and while the client intends to deliver the merchandise or render the services at some subsequent date.

The client also warrants and represents that the account is "free and clear of all liens and incumbrances." That warranty is given to protect the factor from a prior assignment to any other party, from any other previously granted security interest, and from other liens arising by attachment or levy. The existence of a prior lien of any type would, of course, give the factor the right to charge back the purchase price of the account to the client.

Section one contains, as well, one of the most important of the client's warranties and representations in the entire agreement: that the account is owing to the client without defense, offset, or counterclaim. A breach of this warranty by the assertion of a customer claim will give the factor the right to charge back to the client the amount of the purchase price for that account. The client also assigns its interest in the merchandise represented by the receivable, and in any merchandise that might be returned by customers.

Section two. In section two, the factor agrees to purchase all acceptable accounts receivable and to assume the loss on such receivables where the loss arises out of the *financial* inability of the customer to pay; however, this assumption of risk is conditional upon the final acceptance of the merchandise by the client's customer without dispute, offset, or counterclaim. Essentially, this provision is the one that limits the factor's assumption of risk to credit risk only. It also establishes the right of the factor to charge back a purchased account if the client's customer has disputed the liability or has attempted to assert a defense, offset, or counterclaim.

Section two also provides that the amount and terms of all sales be submitted to the factor in advance for approval and that no account be purchased unless actually approved by the factor. Such approval can be withdrawn at any time before actual delivery of the merchandise or the rendition of services. The right of the factor to withdraw approval before delivery is the same right that an unfactored seller would have to stop delivery if such a seller discovered some new financial data about its customer that would dictate a denial of credit.

Section three. Section three provides for a notice to appear on all invoices and bills to the client's customers, explaining that the account has been assigned and is payable to the factor. It is extremely rare to have factoring without notice, because the factor actually keeps a complete ledger of accounts receivable as if it were one of its client's departments. Furthermore, the notice of the assignment provides protection in many areas to the client as well as to the factor.

Section four. In section four, the purchase price is established for the receivables being purchased by the factor. This purchase price is the net amount of the invoices less the commission to the factor, "net amount" being defined in the agreement. The section also requires prior approval of the factor before any credit memo is issued to the client's customer. If a credit is issued or a discount allowed, it may be claimed only by the customer and not by the client at some subsequent date.

In this section the factor is granted an additional possessory security interest in all property or balances to secure any indebtedness which may be owing to the factor, whether such indebtedness arises under the factoring agreement or for any other reason. This type of clause is customary in bank lending agreements as well as in factoring agreements.

Section four also provides for the amount of the advance that the factor may make to its client before the due date of the invoice assigned. In practice, a number of invoices, and sometimes scores of invoices, may be assigned at any given time, and it is the average due date of those invoices that will be calculated as the date when the client would actually be entitled to funds without interest. Any monies remitted to the client before that date would, of course, constitute an advance and would be an interest-bearing advance. In computing interest on an advance, there is usually added to the average due date a number of days for the collection of funds, since it is usual for customers to pay by check and the clearance of checks requires a number of days.

The client, in this section, authorizes the factor to

charge its regular factoring account any obligation which may arise or become owing to the factor by the client. In other words, the account may be charged, not only with items arising under the factoring arrangement, but also with any other type of obligation, including one that may arise from the client's purchase of merchandise from other clients of the factor.

Finally, the client authorizes the factor to remit credit balances at any time and at the factor's discretion. The client will in no event be permitted to pledge the credit of the factor.

Section five. Section five establishes an accounting procedure and specifically states that the credit for the entire month's sales approved and purchased by the factor will be entered on the account on the last day of the month during which such sales were made and assigned.

Section six. Section six contains a provision that the client will maintain a reserve or credit balance with the factor sufficient to protect the factor from the usual types of customer claims, discounts, and returns, as well as other disputed items. Section six also establishes the interest rate under the arrangement, as well as a minimum interest rate, and provides for an escalation or de-escalation of interest depending on the existing prime bank rate from time to time.

Section seven. Section seven provides for a specific assignment of the receivables purchased by the factor together with invoices and conclusive evidence of shipment of merchandise.

Section eight. In section eight, the client warrants that the customer will receive and accept the goods without dispute and without claim, offset, defense, or counterclaim, and will notify the factor promptly if such a claim is made. A dispute may be settled by the factor if such a disputed claim is not actually settled by the client within 60 days after the maturity of the invoice. Returned merchandise, which belongs to the factor, may be resold by the factor at such prices and upon such terms as the factor may in its own discretion determine.

The selling of returns by the factor is exercised only in extremely rare situations, such as in the case of the insolvency of the client. Section eight points out that a chargeback is not to be deemed or constitute a reassignment of an account, and that though a chargeback may be made, title to the account and to the merchandise represented by the account nevertheless remains with the factor until the factor has been compensated for the purchase price advanced to the client. Immediately upon the assertion of a claim or dispute by a customer, the loss shifts by the terms of the agreement from the factor back to the client, even where the customer is ultimately found to be financially unable to pay any part of the obligation.

When checks are received from customers by the client, the client is required to deliver the identical checks to the factor immediately, and all monies and forms of payment shall be endorsed and delivered in kind.

Section nine. Section nine provides for the normal credit terms to be granted by the client to its customers. When additional terms or dating is granted by the client, the commissions to the factor are increased. The reason for this is fairly obvious: the longer the terms, the greater the risk, and the factor is entitled to be compensated for any increased risk. Of course, no increase in terms will be granted without the factor's prior approval. Section nine also provides that where credits are passed or approved the factor will return or credit to its client one-half of the commission applying to that credit.

Section ten. In section ten, the client warrants its solvency. The parties agree that the entire agreement is for the benefit of their successors and assigns, that it cannot be changed orally, and that it represents the complete agreement. The agreement is to be construed in accordance with the laws of a particular state, usually the state in which the factor maintains its principal office.

It is stated that the agreement will continue for a term and will renew automatically unless terminated within a specified period of time. By the agreement, the factor has the opportunity to terminate on shorter notice, and an automatic termination occurs upon the insolvency of the client. The termination, however, does not affect the factor's rights so long as any obligation is open and owing by the client to the factor; all rights and obligations existing prior to termination survive the termination. A jury trial is waived in any action based on the agreement.

7

Standard Factoring Procedures

As DESCRIBED in Chapter 6, the factoring agreement or contract spells out in detail the rights and obligations of both client and factor, is usually effective for at least a year, and defines the commission and interest charges which have been mutually established. Prior to the signing of the contract, certain aspects of the prospective client's operations have been evaluated:

- Customer lists have been examined to determine whether the factor's credit department will be able to accept the credit risk for most of the customers.
- Unusual credit requirements have been discussed and customers' paying habits studied.
- The client's average invoice size has been determined.
- Terms of sale have been analyzed to determine both risk exposure and an estimate of the amount of

funds to be employed in cashing accounts receivable.

- In cases where they are required, programs of seasonal loan support have been discussed, both in form and in amount, and basic agreement has already been reached.

Initial Procedures

After the signing of the contract, several standard operating procedures are initiated. In order to develop these procedures, the factor sends a team of specialists to the client's premises to assist in the smooth transition of routine functions. The client is assigned a client code number for permanent identification by the factor's electronic data processing system; this client code number is to be used on all forms and invoices that are forwarded to the factor.

A General Information form (Exhibit 1) is sent to the client's department heads, outlining procedures to be followed, and checkoff lists are furnished to the client's office personnel. The client's controller, office manager, and head bookkeeper (in some cases all these functions may be the responsibility of one person) are instructed about the forms used for assigning invoices, credits, and allowances. Until new invoices are printed, new clients are supplied with stickers or rubber stamps to apply to customers' invoices, stating that invoices have been sold and should be remitted directly to the factor. A sample invoice is shown in Exhibit 2.

The client is given the name and telephone extension number of the credit man assigned to handle its customers, and the procedures for phoning or mailing customer

Exhibit 1

New Client Instruction Sheet

CHEMICAL BANK - DOMMERICH DIVISION
485 Fifth Avenue
New York, N. Y. 10017

General Information Midstate Manufacturing Co. , Inc.
123 Main Street
Newtown, Pennsylvania

CHARGE SHEETS: Two copies for Chemical Bank - Dommerich Division
      1. Customer's Copy
      2. Assignment Copy
The original invoice and charge sheets should be numbered in consecutive order.
Assignment: Each day's billings should be assigned using the pink assignment
form in duplicate as per specimen herewith attached. The total amount of the
sales for the day and the numbers of charges covering these sales should be
filled in the blank spaces provided therefor in the body of the assignment should
be properly signed by one authorized to do so.
Separate totals should be carried for debits and credits. New totals should be
started at the beginning of each month.
All bills are to be sent to Chemical Bank - Dommerich Division for mailing,
together with the two copies and pink assignment of sales mentioned above.
CREDIT SHEETS: Two copies for Chemical Bank - Dommerich Division
      1. Customer's Copy
      2. Approval Copy
The original credit bill and credit sheets should be numbered consecutively.
All copies sent to Chemical Bank - Dommerich Division should be stamped "Credit. "
All credits should show the date and terms of the bill to which the credit applies.
Approval: Each batch of credits sent to us should be accompanied by a white approval
slip in duplicate as per form enclosed, properly filled in and signed.
RECEIPTS: Receipts and Bills of Lading are to be sent to Chemical Bank - Dommerich
Division and should bear in large figures the bill numbers to which they apply.
CODE: Your code will be . . 3600. . .and should appear on the assignment of sales (pink copy)
as well as credit approval (white copy).
NOTE: Provisions should be made for as many extra copies as may be required by
your customer.
REQUESTS FOR REMITTANCES: Please send your requests for remittances twenty-
four hours before they are needed whenever possible. Requests received after
1 P.M. New York time will not be acted upon until the following business day.
Whether you write, telegraph or telephone, kindly include the net amount of your
sales, (less credits) for the month to that date.
      For example: Request $20,000. Net Sales $24,000.
CLOSING DATE: Our closing date is the second working day of the month and all sales
of a previous month received by us after this date will be accounted for to you in
the following month.
CORRESPONDENCE: Kindly address all correspondence to Chemical Bank - Dommerich
Division.

orders to the factor are explained in detail. The client is
then introduced to key operating personnel so that it will
know the appropriate person to contact for all requirements. Usually all these procedures and visits are handled
under the supervision of the factor's account executive
who will be handling the general affairs of the client.

Exhibit 2

Sample Invoice with Legend of Payment Imprinted

Midstate Manufacturing Co. , Inc.
123 Main Street
Newtown, Pennsylvania

DATE June 6, 1969

BILL NO.   408

SOLD TO

┌ Ridgeville Department Store
645 West 4th Street
Wagner, Texas   ┐

ORDER NO. 16A

SHIPPED VIA Air Freight

└   ┘

TERMS Net 10 EOM

This Account has been Assigned to, is Owned by, and is Payable in New York Funds at par to
CHEMICAL BANK N. Y. TRUST CO. – DOMMERICH DIVISION
485 FIFTH AVENUE, NEW YORK, N. Y. 10017
If this account is not found to be correct in all respects Dommerich Division must be notified at once

PIECE NO.	YARDS	DESCRIPTION	PRICE	AMOUNT	TOTAL
4	100	White Satin	$2.55 per yd.		$255.00

NO CREDITS OR DEDUCTIONS WILL BE ALLOWED UPON THIS BILL UNLESS NOTICE OF CLAIM THEREFOR IS MADE WITHIN 10 DAYS AFTER RECEIPT OF GOODS TO CHEMICAL BANK N. Y. TRUST CO. – DOMMERICH DIVISION. AND SAME CONSENTED TO BY THEM.
GOODS DELIVERED TO COMMON CARRIERS ARE AT THE RISK OF THE PURCHASER

Within the factor's own organization, all department heads are notified of the existence of the new client and are furnished written summaries of all pertinent details necessary for the effective handling of the client's affairs. Special handling instructions, deviations from normal procedures, vital statistics—all are included on the summary. Deposit slips are then obtained from the client so that the factor can deposit funds, when requested, directly into the client's bank account.

Mechanics of Processing a Client Order

For a better understanding of the day-to-day procedures, it is helpful to examine the metamorphosis of a typical client order into a completed transaction. First, the client's office calls the factor's order board requesting credit approval for a customer's order. The customer's name and address, the terms and amount of the order, and the approximate delivery date are furnished to the order board clerk, who fills out a slip listing this information (see Exhibit 3). If the order is to be shipped a month or more later, a special form is sent to the factor (see Exhibit 4).

The slip is then given to a file clerk, who pulls the customer's credit file and gives the file and the request to the appropriate credit man. If the order is approved, the credit man initials the slip and assigns a credit approval serial number. If the order cannot be approved, the client is informed that the shipment will be made at the client's own risk (see Exhibit 5). This process may take from five minutes to several days, depending on the availability of adequate credit information in relation to the size and terms of the order, and on the status of the customer's obligation, if any, to the factor. The approval slip is then returned to the order board, where a clerk phones the client on a direct telephone line and gives the credit approval serial number.

Some time later, when the merchandise ordered is shipped by the client, the client's office prepares an original and duplicate invoice showing the approval number, along with an assignment schedule, and forwards this material along with evidence of shipment to the factor's office. The original invoice bearing the notice of assignment to the factor is mailed to the customer, and the duplicate copy used for posting to the factor's accounts receivable ledger. At the same time, the client's account with the factor is credited with the net amount of the transaction, just as if the client had made a deposit to its account in the bank.

Exhibit 3

Credit Approval Form

DOMMERICH DIVISION
Chemical Bank New York Trust Company
485 FIFTH AVE. NEW YORK, N.Y. 10017
CREDIT OFFICE-ORDER APPROVAL
DATE 6/6/69

Midstate Manufacturing Co., Inc.
123 Main Street
Newtown, Pennsylvania

ACCOUNT CODE 3620

CUSTOMER CODE NO.	CUSTOMER NAME AND ADDRESS	TERMS	DELIVERY	AMOUNT APPROVED	CHECKED BY	CREDIT APPROVAL NO.	DATE REC'D	CREDIT INFO.
	Ridgeville Department Store	Net 10 EOM	July 15, 1969	$3,000		67		
	645 West 4th Street							
	Wagner, Texas							

TERMS AND CREDIT PASSED SUBJECT TO FINAL APPROVAL AT TIME OF DELIVERY

Exhibit 4

Credit Approval Form Where Product Is to Be Delivered a Month or More Later

REQUEST FOR CREDIT APPROVAL

Ridgeville Department Store
(CUSTOMER)

CLIENT MIDSTATE MANUFACTURING CO. INC.

645 West 4th Street

DATE June 6, 1969

Wagner, Texas

TERMS N/10 E.O.M. DELIVERY by July 15, 1969 AMOUNT $3,000

DOMMERICH DIVISION-CHEMICAL BANK N.Y. TRUST CO.
485 FIFTH AVENUE. NEW YORK, N.Y. 10017

CREDIT DECISION:
DATE: _____

Upon receipt of the customer's remittance, the transaction is closed out on the factor's book. If payment on a due invoice is not made within a reasonable time from the posted due date, the factor's collection department makes contact with the customer by statement (Exhibit 6), let-

Exhibit 5

Credit Rejection Form

CHEMICAL BANK NEW YORK TRUST COMPANY
Dommerich Division

485 FIFTH AVENUE
NEW YORK, N.Y. 10017
(212) 986-5300

Midstate Manufacturing Co. , Inc.   March 6, 1969
_____   _____
Client   Date

Gentlemen:

Kindly note that the sales listed below have not been approved by us as to credit. Shipments have been made and the items have been billed and entered on our books for your account and at your sole risk. If this is not in accordance with your understanding, please notify us at once.

Customer	Inv.Date	Inv. No.	Terms	Amount
Ridgeville Dept. Store	2/25/69	127	Net 10-EOM	$1,255.00

Very truly yours,

CHEMICAL BANK NEW YORK TRUST COMPANY
DOMMERICH DIVISION

_____
Credit Department

Exhibit 6

IBM Statement of Customer's Account

TEL. 212 - 986 - 5300

DOMMERICH DIVISION
CHEMICAL BANK NEW YORK TRUST COMPANY
485 FIFTH AVE., NEW YORK, N.Y. 10017
STATEMENT

CUSTOMER'S COPY

SOLD TO:

CUSTOMER NO. 65732   DATE 5/31/69   PAGE NO. 1

Ridgeville Dept. Store
645 West 4th Street
Wagner, Texas

IMPORTANT
INDICATE CUSTOMER NUMBER AND SUPPLIER'S
NAME ON ALL CORRESPONDENCE

MIDSTATE MANUFACTURING CO., INC.

INVOICE NUMBER	C/T	STORE NO.	INVOICE DATE	AS OF DATE	TERMS	SUPPLIER TYPE TRANSACTION	EXTRA DATING	1st DUE DATE	FINAL DUE DATE	DAYS LATE	DEBIT AMOUNT	CREDIT AMOUNT	TRANS. CODE
408	1		6/6/69	--	10 EOM			7-10-69			$255.00		

PLEASE RETURN THIS STATEMENT
WITH YOUR REMITTANCE TO

$255.00

DOMMERICH DIVISION CHEMICAL BANK NEW YORK TRUST COMPANY
485 FIFTH AVE., NEW YORK, N.Y. 10017

IF YOUR REMITTANCE HAS ALREADY BEEN MADE
PLEASE DISREGARD.
NOTIFY US OF ANY DISCREPANCIES ON THIS
STATEMENT.

INTEREST WILL BE CHARGED ON PAST DUE ACCOUNTS

ter, or phone, depending upon the amount of the bill, the location of the customer, and the extent of the payment delinquency. The client has no involvement in the transaction once the customer's order is accepted, shipped, and billed.

Accounting Treatment of the Factor/Client Relationship

When a company enters into a factoring agreement, there are financial and bookkeeping considerations, other than the day-to-day activities, that must be considered. Certain differences are evident on the client's financial statement after factoring. The balance sheet no longer shows any trade receivables, because the client has sold them. They now belong to the factor, and the client has no beneficial interest in them. A receivable from the factor replaces these trade receivables and is generally much smaller, since advances from the factor are direct reductions against this receivable. The payables are proportionately smaller, because a predictable source of funds is now available to pay owings as they mature, or prior to maturity if cash flow permits. With the greater availability of cash, trade liabilities may be kept lower than before, consequently improving the current ratio.

Factoring has no other direct effect upon the client's statements. The Statement of Income is affected only by a potentially faster turnover of goods, generated by a greater availability of funds. No special tax considerations are involved, and all other loans are unaffected except that the collateral availability is reduced by the trade receivables, which now belong to the factor. It is highly unlikely, except in unusual cases, that a commercial bank will make an unsecured loan to a company cashing its receivables with a factor. On the other hand, a bank will regard favorably an unsecured loan to a company which factors on a maturity basis, since all the company's accounts are guaranteed as to credit, and the collection dates are known in advance from the factor's account current statement.

When auditing a client who is factored, the accountant must quickly learn all he can about the methods of a factor, and the best way to do this is to read thoroughly the client's factoring contract (see Chapter 6 on the factoring contract). However, there are certain expressions and terms, unique to factoring, which the client's accountant must be aware of and understand.

Average due date—maturity date. This date is significant: the settlement date when the factor will pay its client for the month's sales. Any monies paid before this date will be subject to the interest rate called for in the contract. If payment is not wanted by the client at the maturity date, it is generally transferred to a "lesser interest account" where interest is credited to the balance at a rate approximately equal to the bank "prime rate."

The average due date is computed by a specific method. Each invoice is examined separately. The number of days from the end of the account current month to the due date of the invoice is multiplied by the face amount of the invoice. The resulting number is referred to as a dollar day unit. A total is then made of the sales and dollar day units.

Now each credit is examined and the due date of the original invoice is determined. Again the number of days from the end of the month to the unmatured due date of the original invoice is computed, and this figure is multiplied by the face amount of the credit. This result will be a negative dollar day unit. Credits may also be issued for invoices which already are past due. The dollar day units on these items are charges and not credits.

The net sales total for the month and the net dollar day units give an average time. The contractual collection day period is added to this total, and the result is the average due date of the month's sales. The following statement will illustrate a portion of a hypothetical account current worksheet for the month of May.

Invoice Date	Terms	Amount	Due Date	Days From 5-31	Dollar Day Units
5–6	Net 60	$ 3,000	7–5	35	105,000
5–12	Net 10	10,000	5–22	(9)	(90,000)
5–18	Net 90	8,000	8–16	77	616,000
5–19	Net 60	6,000	7–18	48	288,000
5–22	Net 60	6,000	7–21	51	306,000
		$33,000			1,255,000

Credit Date	Invoice Due Date	Amount	Days	Dollar Day Units
5–18	4–1	$(6,000)	(60)	360,000
5–27	7–5	(1,000)	35	(35,000)
		$ 7,000	60	1,550,000
		$26,000		

Prime rate. The interest rates of the factor/finance company are somewhat higher than those of a bank. One reason is that the factor/finance company, in a given situation, is lending a proportionately higher amount of money. Then again, it may be lending money to a borrower to whom credit is not otherwise available.

Factors' contracts provide for interest at a specific rate with increases and decreases based upon the so-called prime rate, which is the lowest rate that the commercial banks will charge their most favored clients. Usually each increase in the prime rate of 0.5 percent will call for an increase by the factor of 0.6 percent. This apparent differential of 0.1 percent is not unjustified. The banks insist that their borrowers maintain cash balances amounting to 20 percent of their loans, and thus a 0.5 percent increase in the cost of money will cost the factor 0.6 percent. Like all other businessmen, the factor must pass along this extra cost of doing business.

Most factoring companies charge an interest rate that is pegged to the New York bank prime rate. For example, given a bank prime rate of 5 percent per annum, most factoring companies will charge an effective interest rate of 7.8 percent. For every 0.5 percent increase in the prime rate, the factor's interest rate increases by 0.6 percent. Conversely, every drop in the prime rate of 0.5 percent below the current prime rate results in a decrease of 0.6 percent in the factor's interest charge until the factor's effective rate reaches a minimum of 6 percent per annum.

The factored client draws only the money it needs on a daily, a semiweekly, or a weekly basis. Maintenance of a cash bank balance is not required, and therefore interest is paid only on the exact amount of money employed. Since the factor charges interest on advances only to the average due date of the client's receivables, not to the collection date, the client is not penalized by slow-paying customers. If it carried its own receivables, the slow-paying customer would cost it money, and it would be forced to borrow a greater amount of funds from the bank to cover the monies not collected on the due date. Factors do, however, add a number of days (usually five to ten) to the average due date to compensate for normal delay of mails and bank clearance of checks.

Real cost of bank borrowing. There is an assumption held by many businessmen that the interest rates charged by the factor are much higher than the rates charged by the bank. To a large extent, this assumption is based on the fact that the stated interest rate charged by the bank is lower than that of the factor. However, this simple answer overlooks some matters that affect the actual rate of interest.

Let us assume that a company is borrowing on an "own paper" basis from a bank at a stated rate of interest of approximately 6 percent per annum. But commercial banks usually require borrowers to maintain compensating balances of 15 to 20 percent of the amount borrowed, and in many cases commercial banks require the maintenance of compensating balances whether or not the customer is actually borrowing the funds held available. In addition, when the customer borrows, the bank normally discounts the note. This means that the customer only gets the use of the gross amount less the interest charge that is deducted at the time of the loan. Nevertheless, the customer is paying the stated interest rate for the gross amount borrowed. He is also not able to utilize the amount of funds that must lie idle in his bank account as a compensating balance. These two elements raise the effective borrowing rate to 7.54 percent per annum.

The need for cash must also be considered when weighing interest rates. The customer normally borrows from the bank on a 90-day note. But does the borrower actually require the full amount over the entire duration of the note? Rarely. During the course of the business month, there are periods when collections are heavy and when outgoing payments may be lower than average. During these periods he is paying for the full amount borrowed, but uses a substantially smaller amount. At the same time, he receives no interest for his larger cash balances, which might help offset his borrowing costs. At a factor, the client draws funds only as needed, and interest is charged on the amount owed daily. It is possible that, where there is a wide variance in the need for funds, the real interest cost would be lower at a factor.

Department risk items. Credit risk is not accepted for invoices that have not been approved by the factor's credit department. Such invoices are accepted on "department risk" or "client risk," and the factor makes every effort to collect the amount owed. However, if the account proves uncollectible, the amount owing is charged back to the client and deducted from the factor's remittance to its client.

Factor's acceptance of risk. The typical factoring contract contains a clause to the effect that the factor assumes the loss on receivables due to the *financial inability of the customer to pay*. This simply means that if the customer has the resources to pay and does not, then any unpaid balance of a financially solvent company is the client's responsibility. This is a standard clause to prevent the factor from being "caught in the middle" in a merchandising dispute or any conflict on the nature of the goods sold or the terms of delivery. In actual practice, as soon as the customer notifies the factor of a claim for damaged or improper merchandise, short shipment, or price adjustment for allowance, the factor immediately informs the client (see Exhibit 7) so that a credit can be issued or the dispute resolved between the client and the customer. Open claims are usually kept on the factor's books for two months, and if they are not resolved by then, they are charged back to the client's account.

Many accounting firms performing their certified audits request confirmation of balance due from (or to) the factor and fail to request details on open department risk items and open claims. These amounts are often quite material, and their omission from the auditor's report could significantly distort sales, bad debts, and retained earnings.

Account current. The account sales department credits the client's account for invoices received, issues checks to the client upon request, and debits the client's account for advances made. At the end of each month, the department prepares an exact account current statement (see Exhibit 8) of the entire month's transactions between client and factor, adding the factor's commission and interest charges and showing the exact status of the client's account as of the month's end. This statement is forwarded to the client for its permanent record. The following will

Exhibit 7

Dispute Notice Sent to Client

DATE__June 6, 1969__

CHEMICAL BANK
Dommerich Division
485 FIFTH AVENUE • NEW YORK, N. Y. 10017

DISPUTE NOTICE

TO:

⌐ Midstate Manufacturing Co. , Inc. ⌐
123 Main Street
Newtown, Pennsylvania

L   ⌐

THE BELOW NAMED CUSTOMER HAS REFUSED PAYMENT OF THE FOLLOWING INVOICE(S) BECAUSE OF A DISPUTE.

CHEMICAL BANK
Dommerich Division

BY_____

CUSTOMER: Ridgeville Department Store

ADDRESS: 645 West 4th Street
Wagner, Texas
TOTAL AMOUNT IN DISPUTE $125. 30

DATE OF INVOICE	INVOICE NUMBER	GROSS AMOUNT	EXPLANATION OF DISPUTE
2/5/69	402	$125.30	Customer claims merchandise was damaged when received.

ANY UNSETTLED PART WILL BE CHARGED BACK TO YOUR ACCOUNT IN **60 DAYS** FROM ABOVE DATE. WILL YOU KINDLY ARRANGE FOR IMMEDIATE SETTLEMENT.

Exhibit 8

Account Current Statement

MONTHLY STATEMENT

3620-0 MIDSTATE MANUFACTURING CO., INC. IN ACCOUNT WITH DOMMERICH DIVISION
123 MAIN STREET CHEMICAL BANK NEW YORK TRUST COMPANY
NEWTOWN, PENNSYLVANIA 485 FIFTH AVE., NEW YORK, N.Y. 10017

May 31, 1969   PAGE NO. 1

DATE	NUMBER	EXPLANATION	INT. DAYS				DEBIT	CREDIT
4/30/9		OPENING BALANCE 4/30/9 INTEREST @ 07.8% TO END OF MONTH	28					$ 58,522.8
5/31/9	1110-0	GROSS SALES LESS RETURNS EQUALS NET SALES				$167,487.82		167,487.8
5/31/9	1110-0	AVERAGE DUE DATE 7/08/9 INTEREST TO AVERAGE DUE DATE					$ 2,496.43	
5/31/9	1110-0	COMMISSION ON SALES 1-92 DAYS @ 1.25%				176,568.42	2,207.11	
		COMMISSION ON D/R SALES 1-92 DAYS @ 1.25%				834.69	10.43	
		REFUND OF COMMISSION ON CREDITS 1-92 DAYS @ .625%			$ 9,915.29			61.9
5/31/9	1110-0	INTEREST ON COMMISSION	15				7.01	
5/31/9		OTHER CHARGES TRANSPORTATION ITEMS CHARGED TO YOUR ACCOUNT AS PER OUR NOTICE FOR THE CURRENT MONTH					8.39 3,821.48	
5/03/9	6454	ADVANCE	25	2,000.00	10.83			
5/07/9	7339	ADVANCE	21	5,000.00	22.75			
5/10/9	6505	ADVANCE	18	56,855.44	221.74			
5/11/9	7397	ADVANCE	17	4,000.00	14.73			
5/15/9	6556	ADVANCE	13	1,000.00	2.82			
5/16/9	7419	ADVANCE	12	1,000.00	2.60			
5/17/9	7422	ADVANCE	11	1,500.00	3.58			
5/18/9	6585	ADVANCE	10	5,000.00	10.83			
5/24/9	6635	ADVANCE	4	3,000.00	2.60			
				79,355.44	292.48			
		TOTAL					79,647.92	
		GRAND TOTALS					88,198.77	226,427.
5/31/9		CLOSING BALANCE					***	138,228.8

THIS ACCOUNT SHALL BE DEEMED ACCEPTED BY YOU, UNLESS WE RECEIVE NOTICE TO THE CONTRARY WITHIN 30 DAYS FROM DATE HEREOF - SUBJECT, HOWEVER, TO ANY AND ALL REDUCTIONS FOR RETURNS, ALLOWANCES, CLAIMS, DISPUTES, COUNTERCLAIMS, SET-OFFS ETC. E. & O.E.

4775

96

present in greater detail the various subdivisions of the account current statement.

- Interest on opening balance: Interest is charged or credited for the full month on the opening balance in the account.
- Net sales: Sales are credited to the account net of all returns and discounts.
- Interest to average due date: Interest is computed for the period from the end of the current month to the average due date at the contract interest rate.
- Commissions on factored sales: The typical contract calls for a set commission rate, but usually has an escalation clause for sales in excess of a specified term. Thus the contract may call for a 1.5 percent commission for sales up to 90 days, and on all sales in excess of 90 days a 25 percent increase in rate for each additional 30 days. As the credit risk is extended for a longer time, the factor seeks extended reimbursement.
- Advances: Any advances taken during the month are reflected here. Interest is charged from the date of the advance until the end of the month.

Exhibit 8 is a typical account current for the month of February. This format of account current is rendered to a client that is not on a maturity basis but requires advances prior to the maturity date of its receivables. Therefore, it is always credited on its opening balance and charged to the due date of its sales. If the client is on a maturity basis, no interest is charged or credited, and the client is paid on the average due date of its sales, in this case May 8.

The closing balance of the prior month of $58,522.81 owed to the client is brought forward and interest is credited at the contract rate of 7.8 percent per annum for the full 28 days of February. The sales net of all returns of $167,487.82 are credited to the client. In this example, the client does not have discounts in his invoices. If there were any discounts, they would be shown and deducted from the sales. The average due date is then computed separately, as described above, and the total number of days determined is shown here as May 8. Interest at 7.8 percent per annum for 69 days on $167,487.82 of sales is determined to be $2,496.43.

The commission rate for this client is 1.25 percent for the first 92 days, both on invoices where the risk is accepted and on department risk invoices. Since no invoices carry dating past 92 days, the escalation commission clause is not in effect. The contract calls for a rebate of one-half the commission rate on credits; this partial rebate takes into account the exposure maintained by the factor until these credits are received. In this case the rebate is .625 percent on the $9,915.29 of credits, or $61.97. Interest on the net commission of $2,155.57 is charged for half a month or 15 days at the contract interest rate.

Transportation of freight claims amounting to $8.39 deducted by the customer on his remittance are charged back to the client. In addition, unresolved merchandise claims of $3,821.48 are charged back to the client. Each advance is shown separately and the interest to the end of the month is charged at the contract interest rate.

Cost of Factoring

In examining the total cost of factoring, the borrower must keep in mind that it is not always the interest cost that is most important (ruling out rates that are patently excessive). Nothing can be more important than obtaining the size of loan needed to run a business on its most profitable level. The inability to obtain an adequate amount of money can not only stifle growth but also depress earnings to a point where, in view of the time and effort expended in a business, there is little point to continue in operation.

Rate of commission. The basic factoring fee is a commission charged on the net volume of sales factored, usually 1 to 1.5 percent. The actual rate of commission is negotiated with each client on the basis of the dollar volume of sales, the character and quality of the client's customers, the normal terms of sale, and the average unit size of the client's invoices. The client that factors a larger volume will usually pay a lower rate of commission than a comparable client whose volume is significantly smaller. And the client dealing with customers whose risk of insolvency is high and from whom it is difficult to collect will be charged a higher rate of commission. The time element is still another consideration. If the terms of the sale average 30 days, the factor assumes less of a risk exposure than if terms extend over a 3- or 4-month period.

A particularly important consideration is the average unit size of the invoice. Let us examine the case of a client doing an average volume of $1 million. Its normal terms are 30 days and the average invoice size is $500. The client has sales of approximately $90,000 a month. The factor advances 90 percent against sales, so that it has an average investment of nearly $80,000 each month. To handle this volume the factor will process and post 2,000 invoices annually and a somewhat lesser number of payments, since each customer's payments usually apply against an average of two of three originally issued invoices. This client is charged a commission of 1 percent of net sales, so that the factor earns a gross commission income of $10,000.

This same factor has a comparable client that also does an annual volume of $1 million; however, its average invoice size is only $250. In addition, this client extends terms to its customers that average 60 days from the date of invoice. This means that the factor will be employing $160,000 on the average and will be processing 4,000 invoice units during the year. Obviously, it would be unsound business practice for the factor to apply the same 1 percent commission that it charged the first client. The factor would be earning the same amount of commission income for advancing twice as much money, for handling twice as many invoices, and for doubling its credit exposure.

Factoring and the cost of doing business. Paying the factor a commission rate does not really commensurately increase the cost of doing business for the client. Let us look at a hypothetical case that is fairly typical of many businesses. The client does an annual volume of $3 million. Before he employs the professional services of a factor he absorbs the following costs:

1. Accounts receivable bookkeeping requires the services of two people at a combined salary of $10,000 per year.
2. Credit checking requires the major portion of the attention of either a principal of the company or a separate credit manager. In tangible terms the company puts the yearly cost of this function at $7,500.
3. The establishment and maintenance of credit agency facilities reports and collection services cost $2,500.

4. Despite the expenditures for categories 2 and 3, bad debt losses averaged over a three-year period cost the company $5,000 per year.

The total cost of these functions performed by the company comes to $25,000 a year. With luck, this annual cost to the company could shrink somewhat, but there is no guarantee that it will not increase instead, or that bad debts will remain at $5,000 for an indeterminate length of time.

Faced with this cost analysis, the company decides to turn over its sales to a factor at a commission rate of 1 percent. It now substitutes the predictable cost of $30,000 for the $25,000 of costs which the operation formerly had to absorb. For the difference of $5,000 in annual cost, the client receives many actual benefits. Its sales force is freed from concern about bad debt loss on customer's accounts receivable, and can concentrate on selling more products to each customer. Accounts receivable bookkeeping is now processed on electronic data processing equipment, reducing the possibility of human errors, time loss through personnel illness, or other internal problems. And if the client wishes, it can utilize the sophisticated electronic systems of the factor to obtain sales analyses, salesmen's commission reports, and other pertinent data.

Because of the factor's credit department and the large amount of information available to it either through its files or through its extensive credit information gathering services, the factor is able to extend larger lines of credit to customers than the client would or could on its own responsibility. As a financial institution known to many of the client's customers, the factor can obtain information and details from a customer who might be reluctant to divulge this data to a supplier. Possessing larger resources than the client, the factor is also more willing to assume larger credit exposures. Finally, the excellent credit evaluating facilities of the factor enable the client to expand its volume of business with present customers and even extend its sales into areas beyond its regular markets.

Available cash and sales level. The factor sets no abstract limit on the amount of receivables he will purchase per client. The client's cash availability is related primarily to volume. Most factoring companies will advance up to 85 or 90 percent of the receivables purchased at the time of shipment. The greater the sales level, the greater the cash availability to the client.

The greater flexibility and availability of funds under a factoring arrangement is a most important consideration to a growth company. The slightly higher price paid to obtain funds becomes insignificant if with these funds it can increase its sales and its profitability. And over and above the lending of funds, the services provided by the factor can make a vital contribution to the solid, long-term growth of a company.

8

Modern Factoring
and the Future

WHILE the factor has kept pace with the need of American business for almost instantaneous information, certain changes in the concepts of factoring, which have been relatively stable since their earliest beginnings, have begun to emerge. The Controller of the Currency has ruled that nationally chartered banks may conduct factoring operations and the New York State Superintendent of Banking has opened this field to New York State chartered banks.

Until 1965 only a small number of banks operating outside New York City had established bank-operated factoring divisions. However, in January 1965 one of the largest banks in New York purchased intact Hubshman Factors Corp., an old, well-established factoring/commercial finance company, and set up its acquisition as an integrated special-purpose branch of the bank. This event may have signaled the beginning of a new era in the history of factoring.

Early in 1968 the First Pennsylvania Bank and Trust Co. on a do-it-yourself basis employed experienced factoring executives and set up its own factoring division. Shortly thereafter, the Philadelphia National Bank acquired Congress Factors Corporation as a wholly owned subsidiary. Then, in March 1968, Chemical Bank New York Trust Company acquired L. F. Dommerich and Company, Inc., an old-line factoring company. A few months later Bankers Trust Company, following a similar route, purchased another factor, Coleman and Company, and in January 1969, the Chase Manhattan Bank acquired Shapiro Brothers Factors Corporation. Undoubtedly, we have not seen the end of this trend by large commercial banks to get into the field of factoring and commercial finance.

Commercial Banks and Factoring

The large commercial bank entering the factoring field has certain built-in advantages for gathering new business. The loan officer at each of the hundreds of branches is on the alert for loans which can be made on collateral: against accounts receivable, income-producing assets, inventory, or a combination of two or more types of collateral. Loan applications that have formerly been turned down can now be referred to the specialized division of the bank. No longer does the bank owning a factoring division have to refer potential factoring clients to an outside factoring/finance company.

The large-scale entry of the New York City banks into

the secured lending field also has a national impact, since these banks act as correspondents for thousands of smaller banks throughout the country. Through their national business divisions, the New York banks can offer to banks for whom they act as correspondents both the facilities for handling secured loans and the opportunity to participate in a percentage of the loan with them.

We are already acquainted with the fact that the success of the factoring company rests primarily with its specialized techniques and services, which in turn depend heavily on the availability of highly trained specialists. But the development of the professional client executive, credit and loan specialist, or credit-checking technician requires a long period of training and experience; there is no manpower pool from which the banks can draw to staff their commercial finance departments.

The training and experience of the commercial banker has placed little emphasis on the sphere of secured lending. Yet the keen competition from other institutions servicing this area demands that the bank's factoring/finance divisions supply its clients with flexible service on a split-second basis. The fundamental reasons for the success of the factoring/commercial finance industry have been and continue to be flexibility, quick decisions, and quick action —the independence and responsibility of the individual on the firing line. The availability of the account executive, the knowledgeability of the credit man, and the fast, efficient, well-structured services of their organization are the keys to a good factoring operation.

Intelligent senior management of banks that have acquired factoring companies has recognized the importance of maintaining intact the characteristics that attracted its interest in the first place. In almost all instances, the autonomous nature of the acquired companies has been retained. Policy makers in the parent banks have recognized the fundamental differences between factoring and banking and have allowed their new divisions great freedom and latitude in their day-to-day operations.

Because of the vast human and capital resources of the large banks, the factors may be expected to offer refinements in techniques and services as well as movement into industries where their techniques are relatively unknown. One fact, however, is certain: This specialized field will continue to grow and develop with American industry in the coming years.

Factoring in the Electronic Age

The factoring industry is rapidly becoming more and more of a service organization for its clients. In order for the factor to perform its services, it must make orderly compilations of all data on transactions into historical records, and must do this in such a manner that the important elements of each history are readily accessible for immediate use. Because service costs are a vital aspect of the client/factor relationship, it is important for the factor to find the most efficient means possible of maintaining record-keeping costs at a competitive level, and to look to the most advanced clerical methods and equipment available.

Types of electronic equipment. The electronic accounting machines that were the forerunners of our present-day computers were not widely used in factoring, at first, because of the complexity of the factoring business. However, with the advent of the first small, business-oriented computers, the factoring business began installation of card systems. This method, although a great deal faster than other machine or clerical operations, was slow and difficult to control because of the possibility of misplaced cards. Large volumes of cards became unwieldy, and each card was limited in its record size to an 80-digit capacity. Gradually, cards were replaced with magnetic tape, which provided more speed, accuracy, and control. Furthermore, once the limitations of the card size were removed, more complex types of operations became possible.

On magnetic tape it is possible to keep accounts receivable records up to date on a daily basis with the computer making all computations for claims, discount interest, and anticipation. This daily updating allows the factor to process and deposit cash faster with less chance of incorrect application of cash, and to know the exact standing of each client's receivable control figures each day, with no increase in the cost of operating. Under the card system, and on the previous IBM 1401 and 1460 series computers, memory capacity was limited to 16 thousand positions. On the newer IBM 360/30 series (models in the same cost range) the memory capacity is limited to 65 thousand positions. Therefore, on the newer equipment it is now possible to combine into one operation what were many individual steps and reports.

However, magnetic tape has its shortcomings when compared with a disk file using random access. With magnetic tape you have a reel of tape (average length: 2,400 feet) on which your records are in order. But generally speaking, all reports are printed in a certain sequence, and it is not economical to look for specific answers. For example, let us say that the records are in order by customer number, numbers 000–1000 to 950–9560. To find an answer for customer 940–6230, the computer must wind the tape almost to the end.

A disk file, on the other hand, is similar to a phonograph record with a series of arms like the one arm on a record player. With this equipment, you can go immediately to the area on the record that contains the required information, a process referred to as random access. This method makes direct inquiry possible. What is direct inquiry? It is the ability to get only needed, specific answers and not the complete report necessary with magnetic tape. For example, the credit department of a factor, in order to approve credit for a client's customer, must know its credit rating, its outstanding accounts receivable figures aged, its paying habits, and a high ledger dollar amount. With magnetic tape, it is necessary to prepare a huge bimonthly report of all customers on record, since it is impossible to predict in advance what information will be needed. But with a disk file using random access, the credit department can ask for records on each customer only as it needs them, thereby saving a good deal of expenditure.

The process begins with an inquiry station, which looks like a combined typewriter and television screen. The station is linked by cable to the computer, or, if it is at a distance, by a telephone line. The customer number is keyed into this machine and the answer is simultaneously flashed on the screen. If a typewritten copy is desired, it can be obtained at a speed of 100 words per minute or 1,100 lines per minute at additional cost. This makes it possible to obtain partial automatic credit approval based on certain rules that can be established; on the basis of a good customer rating, the absence of past due items over 90 days, and good paying habits, the computer will approve credit up to some predetermined amount.

As data processing continues to develop and the paperwork burden grows, it becomes increasingly important to produce only the paperwork that is essential for human decision. The "management by exception" principle can be utilized more thoroughly with disk files and direct inquiry. Management by exception in its simplest form is a system of identification and communication that signals the supervisor or executive when his attention is needed, and remains silent when his attention is not required.

New developments. There have been tremendous improvements in business equipment and methods, all having a potential bearing on the ability of the factor to serve its client. And although a great gap still exists between equipment availability and effective utilization, the next three to ten years should produce revolutionary changes in concepts. The development likely to have the greatest apparent impact in the field is direct inquiry to the computer via telecommunications. No matter how far away, clients will have immediate access (by telephone wire) to large-scale, sophisticated, almost inconceivably fast, accurate, and efficient processing equipment at the factor's location. Then there is the growth of the small, efficient business machine, which will directly assist in performance of the client's work and at the same time produce output tape or cards for the factor's processing of client records. Eventually, the further development of optical scanning equipment will drastically reduce key punching and key verification, thus significantly reducing costs of operation. The magazine publishing industry now uses optical scanning for recording payments and new subscriptions, as well as in many other areas. All these changes not only provide practical services on a split-second basis but also contribute to lowering service costs.

An important element to enter the picture is the possibility of universal codes such as Dun & Bradstreet's D-U-N-S number, bank account numbers, magnetic ink character-recognition (MICR) numbers, or other methods instituted by the factor to be utilized by all clients.

Universal codes offer fantastic advantages in the transfer of information from client to factor and factor to client, as well as making internal transfer of information by electronic processes possible. While the coding improvement will be the least dramatic of the changes to the layman (and probably regarded by some as "pain-in-the-neck" details) this is the key to the effective utilization of the other modern systems concepts and efficient, wide-scale use of the newer, more sophisticated equipment. The computer with all its marvels is no better than the information that is fed into it. Good coding or proper identification is a must for good, sound input information.

A universal language. In this connection, it might be well to take a harder look at the advantages of universal coding techniques, first, because of the elimination of duplicate efforts involved and, second, because of what they can do in regard to the performance of the overall system. It is apparent that the client that has its own equipment will be the first to benefit from the use of universally accepted codes. If its equipment is presently handling invoicing and sales, it must code its input in order to utilize its own equipment, and if the codes it uses are not codes acceptable to the factor's equipment, the factor must do the same chore on the same input documents. This is obviously a duplication of effort.

Without universal codes, a language barrier exists between the factor's electronic equipment and that of the client. Although some of the equipment available today can actually "respond" to spoken language translation, the translation of codes is usually a much simpler matter. However, difficulties do exist in translations. For instance, the computer that translated "the spirit is willing, but the flesh is weak" into Russian made it "the whiskey is strong, but the meat is tasteless." Something of the same difficulty can exist in code translations, in addition to the time delay and extra costs involved.

Some survey work has been done to determine the feasibility of using a key word in place of customer coding. This could be a six- or seven-digit word using certain parts of the customer name and address. For example:

Foxwood Sportswear Inc.
311 W. Broadway
New York, N.Y.

would be coded as FOXWBWY. In a test of 300 customers with identical names, there were no duplications of customer key words. However, this has not been practical up to now, because the client seems to make too many mistakes in spelling names or addresses. Also, many customers are known by many trade names that require additional cross-referencing to the main name. The future certainly must hold some better method which will eliminate the costly and timely method of coding for computer identification.

With the language barrier eliminated, the factor's equipment can converse directly with any client's equipment without the necessity of any human help other than the original system setup and programming. Furthermore, it can do it at speeds which compare with human speed in the same relationship that a modern jet airline does with a human foot race. The potential savings in cost, the increase in availability of accurate, timely data, and the decrease in processing time will benefit both factor and client.

The factor's data processing services. Through direct inquiry stations, linking the computer directly to the client's office, the client may participate in sharing the factor's computer. This makes immediate response possible and is particularly important to questions relating to inventory control, production control, and customer service, with no time lost in paper handling or data transportation in either direction. The client on its premises keys in the input information to the computer; the computer updates its records and returns the answers.

It will not be unusual for clients to begin to look to the factor for advice and direct service in electronic data processing. The factor already has records containing information that the client needs to control its business, information that serves as the basis for inventory control by shipments, sales statistics, salesman's commission statements, material necessary for sales projections, market analysis, and more. (Several factoring companies have already developed the necessary software and techniques and are now supplying clients with these reports.) In addition, the factor is probably much more efficient in record-keeping methods and management control reporting. With the advance of the factor into areas of more sophisticated record keeping, the client's demand for more services will no doubt accelerate.

A certain minimum degree of activity in a given application is presently required for economic feasibility. However, this does not mean that a relatively small company may not have a large volume of inventory transactions and a very great need for improved inventory control. There may be a special marketing situation which requires the compilation of extensive detail and its rapid digestion into timely answers for management guidance.

The factor's clients with large volumes ($5 million or more sales per year) who can afford a small computer or the older type of electronic accounting machines are the companies that have the easiest means of obtaining a reduction in their factoring costs. They can most readily provide the factor with sales information in a format that will reduce the factor's processing time and cost, and a reduction of cost to the factor can be passed along in the form of a lower rate for the client. Furthermore, this can work two ways; the factor can return a flow of work to the clients to be processed on their equipment. With the advent of direct inquiry stations and time sharing, clients that now have their own installations can most likely reduce their costs by eliminating their installations and sharing a computer with the factor. In this way they can take advantage of a more costly, sophisticated computer and obtain results that they may not get with the type of equipment that they can afford to buy or lease.

The manufacturer with high shipping peaks that does its own clerical work must maintain a large staff and much equipment during its low periods to be able to process the peaks. For this type of manufacturer, the factor can provide more clerical services at a lower cost without backlog delays than the client can provide for itself. The factor has the type of equipment that is less affected by volume than are manual systems; furthermore, a multitude of peaks at varying intervals becomes almost a straight line. This enables the factor to maintain a fairly constant volume in relation to its staff and equipment while processing many individual peaks and valleys.

The client that does not have (and probably cannot afford) exotic equipment is not left out in the cold. It can share its factor's computer and pay only for the time required. For the average manufacturer that attempts to apply some type of data processing equipment but cannot afford costly systems consultants to install the equipment, the modern factor usually maintains an excellent staff that can assist the client until the installation is complete and operating effectively. The progressive factor should be particularly interested in providing this type of help. Its systems people are best able to guide the client into methods compatible with those overall systems concepts that can accomplish the multifold gains whose potentials have been outlined.

The Future of Factoring

It is apparent that the current economic climate has placed a premium on consolidation, merger, and the resulting development of fewer and larger business units in most areas of business operation. The pressures of ever growing capital requirements, the need for advanced research and development facilities to develop new products and improve old ones, the need for up-to-date and expanded plant facilities, and the need for sophisticated and extensive management personnel have all tended to eliminate the smaller organization and promote the formation of larger and more competitively efficient firms. Does this tend to eliminate the future need for factoring? Not at all.

The modern factor, like its industrial counterpart, has been refining its techniques, developing its personnel, and increasing its electronic sophistication. It is ready to offer the large, well-capitalized business a comprehensive program dealing with many necessary companywide functions, a program priced so advantageously that the potential client must find it attractive.

The expanding use of outside services. Outside servicing by a professional organization has become a fact of business life. Many large companies no longer process their own payroll accounts, finding it cheaper and more efficient to farm out this operation to the highly sophisticated service department of one of the major banks. Many intermediate-size companies rent basic equipment for the purpose of recording important data, but send their records out for processing on the computer of a data processing service bureau.

Why not receive credit analysis, accounts receivable bookkeeping, and collection services from an outside professional? All of these functions have both a tangible and an intangible cost. Personnel, equipment, rent for the space in which the various departments are housed, credit agency reports—these are tangible costs, calculable by management with some degree of accuracy. However, there are other costs difficult to assess specifically. There are, in addition to basic payroll expenditures, certain fringe costs, as well as the real but often uncounted costs involved in dealing with the vagaries and personal problems of additional employees. Furthermore, although a company may maintain a competent and perhaps expensive credit department, this does not guarantee the company against loss from bad debts; although it maintains a well-staffed and alert collection department, not all of its bills are collected.

At the proper price, it is therefore highly attractive to turn these functions over to a professional organization which, because of its specialization, is able to do a more efficient job in these areas than a company's own personnel. In this way, both the tangible and the intangible costs are taken out of the company's premises. For a known and easily calculable cost, the company has purchased complete freedom from bad debt loss and from any responsibility or concern in the areas turned over to the factor, and, as a bonus, the factor can provide significant marketing and accounting information as a by-product of its computer operation. This can be a most attractive possibility to officers of large companies who have little interest in the financing elements of the factoring technique but great interest in the area of specialized servicing.

A burgeoning volume. The traditional areas in which the factors found their clients during the 1950's have yielded fewer new clients during the 1960's, and yet the volume of business factored in the 1960's has grown from $4 billion to $8 billion. Recognition by new industries of the value of factoring, together with the factors' acquisition of fewer but larger clients in the older areas, accounted in great measure for this sizable growth.

The next decade will see even greater growth in the amount of business handled by the factor/finance companies. To be sure, this growth is not inevitable; it requires constant imagination, constant self-examination, constant evolution of newer and more efficient techniques, and a constantly growing pool of experienced and talented people. But it will be achieved. Factoring is a dynamic industry looking back to the past and ahead to the future. As the economy of our country continues to grow, the factor/finance companies will surely grow along with it.

Appendix

Typical Contracts

Exhibit I (see Chapter 2)

SECURITY AGREEMENT (ACCOUNTS RECEIVABLE)

CHEMICAL BANK NEW YORK TRUST COMPANY
Dommerich Division
New York, New York

Gentlemen:

We hereby apply to you for loans and other financial accommodations and in consideration of your extending the same on one or more occasions, the following shall constitute the accounts receivable financing agreement between us.

I. DEFINITIONS. As herein used:

1.1 All terms defined in Articles 1 or 9 of the New York Uniform Commercial Code shall have the meanings given therein unless otherwise defined herein.

1.2 *"Receivables"* shall mean and include all of our accounts, contract rights, instruments, documents, chattel paper and general intangibles, whether secured or unsecured, now existing or hereafter created, and whether or not specifically sold or assigned to you hereunder.

1.3 *"Eligible Receivables"* shall mean and include such Receivables which are and at all times shall continue to be acceptable to you in all respects. Criteria for eligibility shall be fixed and revised from time to time solely by you in your exclusive judgment. In general, a Receivable shall in no event be deemed to be eligible unless: (a) delivery of the merchandise or the rendition of services has been completed; (b) no return, rejection or repossession has occurred; (c) such merchandise or services have been finally accepted by the customer without dispute, offset, defense or counterclaim, and (d) such Receivable continues to be in full conformity with the representations and warranties made by us to you with respect thereto; (e) no more than   days have elapsed from the invoice date; (f) you are, and continue to be, satisfied with the credit standing of the customer in relation to amount of credit extended.

1.4 *"Collateral"* shall mean and include: (a) all of our Receivables and any other items of real or personal property in which we have granted or may in the future grant a security interest to you hereunder or in any supplement hereto or otherwise; (b) all proceeds of any of the foregoing in whatever form, including cash, negotiable instruments and other instruments for the payment of money, chattel paper, security agreements or other documents; (c) all of our right, title and interest in and to the goods or other property represented by or securing any of the Receivables; (d) all of our rights as an unpaid vendor or lienor, including stoppage in transit, replevin and reclamation; (e) all additional amounts due to us from any customer, irrespective of whether such additional amounts have been specifically assigned to you; (f) all guaranties, mortgages on real or personal property, leases or other agreements or property securing or relating to any of the items referred to in subparagraph (a) hereof, or acquired for the purpose of securing and enforcing any of such items.

1.5 *"Customer"* shall mean and include the account debtor with respect to any of the Receivables and/or the prospective purchaser with respect to any contract right, and/or any party who enters into or proposes to enter into any contract or other arrangement with us, pursuant to which we are to deliver any personal property or perform any services.

1.6 *"Obligations"* shall mean and include any and all of our indebtedness and/or liabilities to you of every kind, nature and description, direct or indirect, secured or unsecured, joint and several, absolute and contingent, due or to become due, now existing or hereafter arising, regardless of how they arise or by what agreement or instrument they may be evidenced or whether evidenced by any agreement or instrument, including but not limited to all amounts owing by us to you by reason of purchases made by us from other concerns, factored or financed by you, which amounts, whether or not matured and whether or not disputed, may be charged to our account hereunder, without prior notice to us, and all obligations to perform acts or refrain from taking any action.

II. GRANT OF SECURITY INTEREST.

2.1 To secure the payment and performance of all of the Obligations as hereinafter defined, we hereby pledge and assign to you, and grant to you a continuing general security interest in, all of our Collateral and all of our ledger sheets, files, records and documents relating to the Collateral which shall, until delivered to or removed by you, be kept by us in trust for you and without cost to you in appropriate containers in safe places, bearing suitable legends disclosing your security interest. We hereby agree to execute and deliver to you a bill of sale covering all of said ledger sheets, files, records and documents relating to the Collateral, together with the containers in which the same are kept. Each confirmatory assignment schedule or other form of assignment hereafter executed by us shall be deemed to include the foregoing whether or not same appears therein.

2.2 We will, upon the creation of Receivables, or at such intervals as you may require, provide you with: (a) Confirmatory assignment schedules; (b) copies of Customer's invoices; (c) evidence of shipment or delivery; (d) such further schedules and/or information as you may reasonably require. The items to be provided under this paragraph are to be in form satisfactory to you and executed and delivered to you from time to time solely for your convenience in maintaining records of the Collateral and our failure to give any of such items to you promptly shall not affect, terminate, modify or otherwise limit your lien or security interest in the Collateral. The preparation of any invoices, or the shipment of any merchandise or the performance of any services, if such are done prior to preparation of the invoices, shall operate as and constitute an assignment to you of the Receivables represented thereby, whether or not we execute any specific schedule of accounts or other form of assignment.

III. ADVANCES AND INTEREST.

3.1 You hereby agree to make loans and/or advances and other financial accommodations to us and for our account from time to time in such amounts as may be mutually agreed upon. The amount of such loans outstanding at any one time shall not normally exceed   % of the outstanding amount of Eligible Receivables as herein defined. All loans or advances shall be disbursed by you from your office in the City of New York, shall be charged to our account on your books, and shall be payable on demand at such office.

3.2 Interest on all such loans and/or advances shall be charged at the rate of   Such rate of interest shall be increased or decreased by .3% per annum for each increase or decrease, respectively, of .25% that is hereafter made in the Prime Rate in the New York Federal Reserve District. However, the minimum rate charged by you shall be   . All such interest shall be due and payable on the last day of each calendar month. In the event of non-payment of any such interest when due, you are hereby authorized, at your option, to charge the amount so unpaid to our account as of such last day of such calendar month. All collections shall be applied first to payment of any such unpaid interest.

3.3   You will render to us each month a statement of our account which shall constitute an account stated and shall be deemed to be correct and accepted by and binding upon us unless you receive a written statement of our exceptions within thirty (30) days after such statement has been rendered to us.

IV.   REPRESENTATIONS, COVENANTS AND WARRANTIES.

We hereby make the following represeutations, covenants and warranties which shall be deemed to be incorporated by reference in each confirmatory assignment schedule or other form of assignment submitted by us to you, and shall be deemed repeated and confirmed with respect to each Receivable and/or other item of Collateral as it is created or otherwise acquired by us:

4.1   The execution, delivery and performance hereof are within our corporate powers, have been duly authorized, are not in contravention of law or the terms of our Charter, By-Laws or other incorporation papers, or of any indenture, agreement or undertaking to which we are a party or by which we are bound.

4.2   With respect to the Collateral at the time the Collateral becomes subject to your security interest: (a) we shall be the sole owner of and fully authorized to sell, transfer, pledge and/or grant a security interest in each and every item of said Collateral; (b) as to Receivables, each of them shall be a good and valid account representing an undisputed bona fide indebtedness incurred by the Customer therein named, for a fixed sum as set forth in the invoice relating thereto with respect to an absolute sale and delivery upon the specified terms of goods sold by us, or work, labor and/or services theretofore rendered by us; (c) none of the Receivables is or shall be subject to any defense, offset, counterclaim, discount or allowance except as may be stated in the copy of the invoice delivered by us to you, and each Receivable will be paid in full when due; (d) no agreement under which any deduction of any kind may be granted shall have been or shall thereafter be made by us with any Customer except as indicated in writing to you; (e) all documents and agreements shall be true and correct and in all respects what they purport to be; (f) all signatures and endorsements that appear thereon shall be genuine and all signatories and endorsers shall have full capacity to contract; (g) none of the transactions underlying or giving rise to the Collateral shall violate any applicable state or federal laws or regulations, and all documents relating to the Collateral shall be legally sufficient under such laws or regulations and shall be legally enforceable in accordance with their terms.

4.3   All recording, filing and other requirements of giving public notice under any applicable law or ordinance have been fully complied with and we will from time to time do whatever you may request by way of obtaining, executing, delivering and/or filing financing statements, landlord's or mortgagee's waivers, and other notices, and amendments and renewals thereof, and we will take any and all steps and observe such formalities as you may request, in order to create and maintain a valid first lien upon, pledge of, or paramount security interest in, any and all of the Collateral. You are authorized to file financing statements without our signature as specified by the Uniform Commercial Code to perfect or maintain your security interest in all of the Collateral. All charges, expenses and fees you may incur in filing any of the foregoing, and any local taxes relating thereto, shall be charged to our account and added to the Obligations.

4.4   While this Agreement remains in effect and until payment and/or performance in full of all of the Obligations, the pledge and assignment of, and security interest in, all Collateral hereby granted to you, shall continue in full force and effect. During such period we shall not pledge, sell, assign, transfer or create a security interest in any part of the Collateral or grant any security interest in any of our inventory or fixed assets to anyone other than you, without your prior written consent. We hereby agree to defend the same against any and all persons whatsoever.

4.5   Each Customer, guarantor or endorser is solvent and will continue to be fully able to pay all Receivables on which he is obligated in full when due. All tax payments are current and will remain so. We are not and shall not be entitled to pledge your credit on any purchases or for any purpose whatsoever.

4.6   All balance sheets, earnings statements and other financial data which have been or may hereafter be furnished to you to induce you to enter into this Agreement or otherwise in connection herewith, do or shall fairly represent our financial condition as of the dates thereof and/or the results of our operations for the periods for which the same are furnished. All other information, reports and other papers and data furnished to you are or shall be, at the time the same are so furnished, accurate and correct in all material respects and complete insofar as completeness may be necessary to give you a true and accurate knowledge of the subject matter.

4.7   We hereby irrevocably authorize and direct all accountants and auditors employed by us at any time during the term of this Agreement to exhibit and deliver to you copies of any of our financial statements, trial balances or other accounting records of any sort in their possession, and to disclose to you any information they may have concerning our financial status and business operations.

4.8   We shall give you written notice of each office at which we may keep our records pertaining to accounts and/or contract rights. Except as such notice is given, all such records shall be kept at our address as it appears at the foot of this Agreement.

V.   CUSTODY, INSPECTION, COLLECTION AND HANDLING OF COLLATERAL AND RECORDS.

5.1   We will safeguard and protect all Collateral for your account and make no disposition thereof except in the regular course of business.

5.2   Until our authority to do so is terminated by you (which notice you may give at any time when you in your sole discretion may deem it to be in your best interests to do so), we will, at our own cost and expense but on your behalf and for your account, collect and otherwise enforce as your property and in trust for you, all amounts unpaid on Receivables, and shall not commingle such collections with our own funds or use the same except to pay our Obligations to you. As to all monies so collected, including all prepayments by Customers, we shall receive in trust, and deliver to you in original form and on the date of receipt thereof, all checks, drafts, notes, money orders, acceptances, cash and other evidence of indebtedness. All amounts received by you in payment of Receivables assigned to you are to be credited to the account of the undersigned after allowing five (5) days for collection. At any such termination of our authority, or at any other time and without any cause or notice thereof to us, you shall have the right to send notice of assignment and/or notice of your security interest to any and all Customers or any third party holding or otherwise concerned with any of the Collateral, and thereafter you shall have the sole right to collect the Receivables and/or take possession of the Collateral. Any and all of your collection expenses, including but not limited to stationery and postage, telephone and telegraph, secretarial and clerical expenses and the salaries of any collection men utilized, shall be charged to our account and added to the Obligations.

5.3   We shall maintain books and records pertaining to the Collateral in such detail, form and scope as you shall require. We will mark our ledger cards, books of account and other records relating to the Collateral with appropriate notations satisfactory to you, disclosing that such Collateral has been pledged, sold, assigned, mortgaged and/or transferred to you and/or that we have granted to you a security interest therein.

5.4 At all reasonable times, you shall have full access to, and the right to audit, check, inspect and make abstracts and copies from, our books, records, audits, correspondence and all other papers relating to the Collateral. You shall have the right to confirm and verify all Receivables and do whatever you may deem necessary to protect your interests. You or your agents may enter upon any of our premises at any reasonable time during business hours and from time to time for the purpose of inspecting the Collateral and any and all records pertaining thereto.

5.5 We will, immediately upon learning thereof, report to you: any reclamation, return or repossession of goods; all claims or disputes asserted by any Customer or other obligor; and any other matters affecting the value, enforceability or collectibility of any of the Collateral. We shall not, without your consent, compromise or adjust any of the Receivables (or extend the time for payment thereof) or grant any additional discounts, allowances or credits thereon.

5.6 You shall have the right to receive, endorse, assign and/or deliver in your name or ours any and all checks, drafts and other instruments for the payment of money relating to the Receivables, and we hereby waive notice of presentment, protest and non-payment of any instrument so endorsed. We hereby constitute you or your designee as our attorney with power to endorse our name upon any notes, acceptances, checks, drafts, money orders or other evidences of payment or Collateral that may come into your possession; to sign our name on any invoice or bill of lading relating to any of the Receivables, drafts against Customers, assignments and verifications of Receivables and notices to Customers; to send verifications of Receivables to any Customer; to notify the Post Office authorities to change the address for delivery of mail addressed to the undersigned to such address as you may designate; to do all other acts and things necessary to carry out this Agreement. All acts of said attorney or designee are hereby ratified and approved, and said attorney or designee shall not be liable for any acts of omission or commission, nor for any error of judgment or mistake of fact or law; this power being coupled with an interest is irrevocable while any of the Obligations remain unpaid.

5.7 Nothing herein contained shall be construed to constitute us as your agent for any purpose whatsoever, and you shall not be responsible nor liable for any shortage, discrepancy, damage, loss or destruction of any part of the Collateral wherever the same may be located and regardless of the cause thereof. You shall not, under any circumstances or in any event whatsoever have any liability for any error or omission or delay of any kind occurring in the settlement, collection or payment of any of the Receivables or any instrument received in payment thereof or for any damage resulting therefrom. You may, without notice to or consent from us, sue upon or otherwise collect, extend the time of payment of, or compromise or settle for cash, credit or otherwise upon any terms, any of the Receivables or any securities, instruments or insurance applicable thereto and/or release the obligor thereon. You are authorized and empowered to accept the return of the goods represented by any of the Receivables, without notice to or consent by us, all without discharging or in any way affecting our liability hereunder. You do not, by anything herein or in any assignment or otherwise, assume any of our obligations under any contract or agreement assigned to you, and you shall not be responsible in any way for the performance by us of any of the terms and conditions thereof.

5.8 We will pay when due, all taxes, assessments and other charges lawfully levied or assessed upon any of the Collateral, and if such taxes or other charges or assessments remain unpaid after the date fixed for the payment of same, or if any lien shall be claimed which in your opinion may possibly create a valid obligation having priority over the security interest granted to you herein, you may without notice to us pay such taxes, assessments, charges or claims, and the amount thereof shall be charged to our account and added to the Obligations.

5.9 If any of the Receivables includes a charge for any tax payable to any governmental tax authority, you are hereby authorized in your discretion to pay the amount thereof to the proper taxing authority for our account and to charge our account therefor. We shall notify you if any Receivables include any tax due to any such taxing authority and in the absence of your consent, you shall have the right to retain the full proceeds of such Receivable and shall not be liable for any taxes that may be due from us by reason of the sale and delivery creating such Receivable.

5.10 We shall comply with all acts, rules, regulations and orders of any legislative, administrative or judicial body or official, applicable to the Collateral or any part thereof, or to the operation of our business; provided that we may contest any acts, rules, regulations, orders and directions of such bodies or officials in any reasonable manner which will not, in your opinion, adversely affect your rights or the priority of the lien or security interest in the Collateral provided for herein.

5.11 You shall be privileged at any time and from time to time to employ and maintain in any of our premises a custodian selected by you who shall have full authority to do all acts necessary to protect your interests and to report to you thereon. We hereby agree to cooperate with any such custodian and to do whatever you may reasonably request by way of leasing warehouses or otherwise preserving the Collateral. All expenses incurred by you by reason of the employment of the custodian shall be charged to our account and added to the Obligations.

5.12 All costs and expenses, including reasonable attorneys' fees (15% of the principal and interest involved, if not prohibited by law) incurred by you in all efforts made to enforce payment or otherwise effect collection of any Receivables, as well as all attorneys' fees and legal expenses incurred in instituting, maintaining, preserving, enforcing and foreclosing the security interest in any of the Collateral, whether through judicial proceedings or otherwise, or in defending or prosecuting any actions or proceedings arising out of or relating to your transactions with us, shall be charged to our account and added to the Obligations.

VI. EVENTS OF DEFAULT — ACCELERATION.

Any or all of the Obligations shall, at your option and notwithstanding any time or credit allowed by any instrument evidencing a liability, be immediately due and payable without notice or demand upon the occurrence of any of the following events of default: (a) default in the payment or performance, when due or payable, of any of the Obligations; (b) our failure to pay when due any tax or any premium on any life insurance policy assigned to you as Collateral or on any other insurance policy required to be furnished to you under any supplement hereto or otherwise; (c) our making any misrepresentation, orally or in writing, to you for the purpose of obtaining credit or an extension of credit; (d) our failure, either request by you, to furnish financial information or to permit the inspection of books or records; (e) issuance of an injunction or attachment against any of our property; (f) our breach of any representation, warranty, covenant or agreement herein contained or contained in any other agreement or arrangement now or hereafter entered into between us; (g) our suspension of the operation of our present business, becoming insolvent, or unable to meet our debts as they mature, or our calling any meeting of all or any of our creditors or committing any act of bankruptcy; the filing by or against us of any petition under any provision of the Bankruptcy Act as amended, or if any judgment is rendered or lien filed against us; (h) any change in our condition or affairs (financial or otherwise) or that of any endorser, guarantor or surety for any of the Obligations, that in your opinion impairs your security or increases your risk.

VII. RIGHTS AND REMEDIES AFTER DEFAULT.

7.1 Upon the occurrence of any of the aforementioned events of default and at any time thereafter (such default not having previously been cured), you shall have the right to terminate this Agreement without notice and, in addition to all other rights and remedies, all rights and remedies of a secured party under the New York Uniform Commercial Code, including, without limitation, the right to foreclose the security interest granted herein by any available judicial procedure and/or to take possession of any or all of the Collateral with or without judicial process. For that purpose you may, so far as we can give authority therefor, enter upon any or all of the premises where any of the Collateral may be situated and take possession and remove the same therefrom.

7.2   You shall have the right in your sole discretion to determine which rights, security, liens, security interests or remedies you shall at any time pursue, relinquish, subordinate, modify or take any other action with respect thereto, without in any way modifying or affecting any of them or any of your rights hereunder. Any monies, deposits, Receivables, balances, or other property of ours which may come into your hands at any time or in any manner, may be retained by you and applied to any of the Obligations and to any Obligations of any of our affiliates to you.

7.3   The enumeration of the foregoing rights and remedies is not intended to be exhaustive and the exercise of any right or remedy shall not preclude the exercise of any other rights or remedies, all of which shall be cumulative and not alternative.

VIII.   WAIVERS.

8.1   We hereby waive notice of non-payment of any of the Receivables, demand, presentment, protest and notice thereof with respect to any and all instruments, notice of acceptance hereof, notice of loans or advances made, credit extended, Collateral received or delivered, or any other action taken in reliance hereon, and all other demands and notices of any description, except such as are expressly provided for herein.

8.2   No delay or omission on your part in exercising any right, remedy or option shall operate as a waiver of such or any other right, remedy or option or of any default.

8.3   Each of the parties hereby waives trial by jury in any action or proceeding of any kind or nature in any court to which they may both be parties, whether arising out of, under, or by reason of this Agreement or any assignment, Receivable or other transaction hereunder or by reason of any other cause or dispute whatsoever between them of any kind or nature.

IX.   EFFECTIVE DATE AND TERMINATION; MISCELLANEOUS.

9.1   This Agreement, which shall inure to the benefit of and shall be binding upon the respective successors and assigns of each of us, shall become effective on the day when finally accepted by you at your office in the State of New York, shall be governed, construed and interpreted in all respects in accordance with the laws of the State of New York, and shall continue in full force and effect until one year from the date hereof, and from year to year thereafter, unless sooner terminated as herein provided. We may terminate this Agreement as of the anniversary of its effective date in any year by giving you at least sixty (60) days' prior written notice, and you shall have the right to terminate on 30 days' notice at any time.

9.2   The termination of this Agreement shall not affect any rights of either of us, or any obligation of either of us to the other, arising prior to the effective date of such termination, and the provisions hereof shall continue to be fully operative until all transactions entered into, rights created or Obligations incurred prior to such termination have been fully disposed of, concluded or liquidated. The security interest, lien and rights granted to you hereunder shall continue in full force and effect, notwithstanding the termination of this Agreement or the fact that our account may from time to time be temporarily in a credit position, until all of the Obligations, including but not limited to our liabilities for indebtedness guaranteed by you and/or for withholding taxes, have been paid in full or we have furnished you with an indemnification satisfactory to you with respect thereto. All representations, warranties, covenants, waivers and agreements contained herein shall survive termination hereof unless otherwise provided.

9.3   This Agreement contains the entire understanding between us and any promises, representations, warranties or guarantees not herein contained shall have no force and effect unless in writing, signed by our respective officers. Neither this Agreement nor any portion or provision hereof my be changed, modified, amended, waived, supplemented, discharged, cancelled or terminated orally or by any course of dealing, or in any manner other than by an agreement in writing, signed by the party to be charged.

9.4   We hereby agree that the Supreme Court of the State of New York, in the County of New York, and the United States District Court for the Southern District of New York, shall have jurisdiction to hear and determine any claims or disputes between us, pertaining directly or indirectly to this Agreement or to any matter arising therefrom. Each of us expressly submits and consents in advance to such jurisdiction in any action or proceeding commenced by the other in either of such Courts, hereby waiving personal service of the summons and complaint, or other process or papers issued therein, and agreeing that service of such summons and complaint, or other process or papers may be made by registered or certified mail addressed to the party to be served at the address to which notices are to be sent pursuant to Paragraph 9.5 hereof. Should the party so served fail to appear or answer to any summons, complaint, process or papers so served within thirty (30) days after the mailing thereof, it shall be deemed in default and an order and/or judgment may be entered by the other against it as demanded or prayed for in such summons, complaint, process or papers.

9.5   Any notice to be served on either party hereunder must be served by certified mail addressed to the party to be served at the address shown at the beginning or foot hereof, or to any other address to which the party to be served has authorized the other in writing to send such notices.

9.6   If any part of this Agreement is contrary to, prohibited by, or deemed invalid under applicable laws or regulations, such provision shall be inapplicable and deemed omitted to the extent so contrary, prohibited or invalid, but the remainder hereof shall not be invalidated thereby and shall be given effect so far as possible.

Very truly yours,

_____

By_____

                                                Title

ACCEPTED IN NEW YORK CITY   Address:_____

THIS   DAY OF   19

CHEMICAL BANK NEW YORK TRUST COMPANY—   _____

DOMMERICH DIVISION

By_____

Address:_____

_____

Exhibit II (see Chapter 6)

Factoring Contract

. DOMMERICH & CO., INC.
V YORK, N. Y.

: Sirs:

We are pleased to set forth in this letter the terms of the agreement by which you are to act as our sole factor, effective as of

November 30, 1966

1. We agree to do all of our business through you as our sole factor. The undersigned hereby assigns and sells to you as absolute ers, and you hereby purchase from the undersigned and without recourse to the undersigned except as set forth hereinafter, all accounts, s, bills, acceptances or other forms of obligation (hereinafter collectively termed "receivables") now existing or hereafter created, ptable to you, and which the undersigned represents and warrants to be at the time of assignment to you bona fide and existing obliga- of its customers arising out of the sale of merchandise and/or the rendition of services by the undersigned in the ordinary course of its ness, free and clear of all liens and incumbrances and owned by and owing to the undersigned without defense, offset or counterclaim. eivables not approved by you as provided below in whole or in part shall be assigned to you with full recourse to the undersigned to the nt and in the respects not so approved. The undersigned further sells, assigns and transfers to you all its title and/or interest in the chandise represented by said receivables and in all such merchandise that may be returned by customers and all its right of stoppage in sit, replevin and reclamation and as an unpaid vendor and/or lienor. Any merchandise so recovered shall be treated as returned merchan- and shall be set aside, marked with your name and held for your account as owner. The undersigned shall notify you promptly of all returned merchandise.

2. You agree to purchase all our accounts receivable acceptable to you in accordance with the terms of this agreement, and you assume loss on receivables so assigned to you pursuant to the terms hereof due to the financial inability of the customer to pay, provided the omer has received and finally accepted the merchandise which is the subject of the sale and of the account receivable assigned to and hased by you, without dispute, claim or counterclaim, as provided by our warranty and representation.

The amount and terms of each sale to a customer of the undersigned shall be submitted to you for your approval in writing, and no or deliveries shall be made without such written approval, which may be withdrawn at any time before delivery of the merchandise or ition of the services.

3. All bills and invoices for such accounts as are assigned to and purchased by you hereunder shall show on the face thereof the wing legend: "This account has been assigned to and is owned by and payable only in New York Exchange at par to L. F. DOMMERICH)., INC., 485 Fifth Avenue, New York 17, N. Y., to whom any objection to this bill or its terms must be reported on receipt of same", shall be sent to you ready for transmission to the customers, the postage charge thereon to be borne by us.

4. The purchase price of receivables accepted by you is to be the net amount thereof, less your commission, due and payable at the of purchase, in an amount equal to one and one-half (1 1/2%) percent (%) of said net amount. "Net amount" of receivables means gross unt of said receivables less returns and less discounts, credits or allowances of any nature at any time issued, owing, granted or outstanding. scount, credit or allowance after issuance or granting may be claimed solely by the customer. No discount, credit or allowance will be d or granted by the undersigned to a customer without your consent. You are to pay or credit to the undersigned at your discretion, a up to Eighty percent (80%) of the purchase price and the balance of said purchase price, less any monies remitted or other- advanced by you for the account of the undersigned, including any amounts which you may be obligated to pay in the future, at the thly average due date of said receivables, calculated and construed by you on the basis of the terms of sale given to each customer and ding ten days for collection. You shall be entitled to hold all sums and all property of the undersigned at any time to its credit or in your ession, or upon or in which you may have a lien or security interest, as security for any and all obligations of the undersigned at any time g to you, no matter how or when arising and whether under this or any other agreement or otherwise, and including all obligations for hases made by the undersigned from any other concern factored by you. You shall have the right and are hereby irrevocably authorized directed to charge to the account of the undersigned the amounts of any and all such obligations. Recourse to security shall not at any be required and the undersigned shall at all times remain liable for the repayment on demand to you of all loans and advances to or for account of the undersigned and of all other obligations of the undersigned.

Subject to the provisions of this agreement, at the request of the undersigned you shall remit and at any time in your sole discretion may remit any moneys standing to the credit of the undersigned on your books. The undersigned shall not pledge your credit for any ose whatsoever.

5. You will credit us on the last day of the month with the net amount of the current month's sales approved by you, such credit e as of the average due date of such sales.

6. We shall at all times maintain a credit balance with you commensurate with the volume and character of the business done as rmined by you in your discretion, as a protection to you against all possible returns and claims of our customers. You may make remit- es to us monthly or, if requested, more often, against the available balance to our credit on your books. You will send us an accounting thly in which interest is to be figured as follows: Predicated on a 6 % per annum prime New York City bank rate, interest will be lated at 9 % per annum. On each increase of the prime New York City bank rate by one quarter of one (¼ of 1%) percent, your est rate will be increased by 3 %. On each decrease of the prime New York City bank rate by one quarter of one (¼ of 1%) per- , your interest rate will be decreased by 3 %, but in no event shall the rate of interest hereunder be less than 6% per annum. Any ge in the rate of interest hereunder shall become effective on the 1st day of the month following the month in which the New York prime bank rate shall have been changed. Such monthly accounting shall be deemed accepted by us unless written exceptions thereto served upon you within thirty (30) days after any such accounting is rendered.

7. The undersigned will provide you with an assignment satisfactory to you of receivables purchased, together with copies of omers' invoices and conclusive evidence of shipments, satisfactory to you. Billings on such invoices, by whomsoever done, shall constitute mment thereof to you of the receivables represented thereby, whether or not the undersigned executes any other specific instrument of mment.

8. The undersigned hereby further warrants to you that the customer in each instance has received and will accept the merchandise and/or the services rendered, and the invoice therefor, without dispute, claim, offset, defense or counterclaim. The undersigned will notify promptly of and shall at its own cost and expense, including attorneys' fees, settle all disputes and/or claims and will pay you promptly amount of the receivables affected thereby. Any dispute, claim, offset, defense or counterclaim not settled by us by the sixtieth day next wing the maturity of the invoice affected thereby may, if you so elect, be settled, compromised, adjusted or litigated by you directly with customer or other complainant upon such terms and conditions as you in your sole discretion deem advisable and for our account and risk. may also in your discretion take possession of and sell or cause to be sold, without notice to us, any returned merchandise at such prices, ich purchasers and upon such terms as you deem advisable and in any case to charge the deficiency, costs and expenses thereof, including neys' fees, to the undersigned. In addition to any other right to which you are entitled under this agreement, where there is such dispute

and/or claim, or if any unapproved receivables be unpaid at its maturity, you may charge the amount of the receivable so affected or unpaid to the undersigned; but such charge-back shall not be deemed nor shall it constitute a reassignment thereof, and title thereto and to the merchandise represented thereby shall remain in you until you are fully reimbursed. Regardless of the date or dates upon which you charge back the amount of any receivable, where there is such dispute, claim, offset, defense or counterclaim, the undersigned agrees that immediately upon the occurrence of any such dispute, claim, offset, defense or counterclaim, you shall no longer bear the loss on such receivables due to financial inability of the customer to pay, and such loss shall immediately revert to and be assumed by the undersigned without any act upon your part to effect the same. In the event of any breach by the undersigned of any provision and/or upon the termination of this agreement the undersigned will repay upon demand all obligations to you of the undersigned and in addition thereto all costs and expenses incurred including a reasonable allowance for attorneys' fees, to obtain or enforce payment of any obligation of the undersigned to you, or in prosecution or defense of any action or proceeding either against you or against the undersigned, concerning any matter growing out of connected with this agreement and/or the receivables assigned and/or any obligations of the undersigned to you. If any remittances are made directly to the undersigned, the undersigned shall hold the same as your property and immediately deliver to you the identical checks, money or other forms of payment received and you shall have the right to endorse the name of the undersigned on any and all checks or other forms of remittance received, where such endorsement is required to effect collection. If at any time you shall be required to pay any state, county, local or federal sales or excise taxes on sales hereunder, the undersigned will repay to you the amount of tax so paid by you.

9. Commissions payable to you hereunder are based upon our usual and regular terms, which do not exceed Ninety days. On sales on which additional terms or dating are granted, your commissions thereon shall be increased at the rate of twenty-five percent (25% of the basic commission rate, for each additional thirty (30) days or fraction thereof by which our regular terms are increased. No such increase in terms, however, shall be granted without your written approval. When credits are passed you will rebate to us one-half of commission applying to such credits.

10. The undersigned hereby warrants its solvency. This agreement is entered into for the benefit of the parties hereto, their successors and assigns, and cannot be changed, modified or terminated orally. It is the complete agreement between the parties. This agreement, made in the State of New York, shall be interpreted according to the laws of said State and shall continue in full force and effect until one year from the effective date hereof and from year to year thereafter unless terminated by you or unless the undersigned notifies you of its desire to terminate this agreement on its anniversary date in any year by giving you at least sixty days' prior written notice. Notwithstanding such notice by the undersigned, this agreement shall nevertheless continue in full force and effect as to, and be binding upon, the undersigned after such anniversary until the undersigned has fully paid and satisfied all of its obligations to you, no matter how or when arising and whether under this or any other agreement or otherwise. You shall have the right to terminate this agreement at any time upon sixty days prior written notice. Termination shall be effected by the mailing of a registered letter of notice addressed by either of us to the other, and the termination shall be effective as of the date so fixed in such notice. Notwithstanding the foregoing, should either of us become insolvent or unable to meet its debts as they mature or commit an act of bankruptcy, the other of us shall have the right to terminate this agreement at any time without prior notice. The rights and obligations arising out of transactions having their inception prior to the termination, shall be affected and all of the terms, conditions and provisions hereof shall continue to be fully operative until all transactions entered into rights created or obligations incurred hereunder prior to the termination have been fully disposed of, concluded and/or liquidated. You are the undersigned do hereby waive any and all rights to a trial by jury in any action or proceeding arising herefrom or based hereon. No delay or failure on your part in exercising any right, privilege or option hereunder shall operate as a waiver of such or of any other right, privilege or option, and no waiver whatever shall be valid unless in writing signed by you and then only to the extent therein set forth.

ATTEST:

MIDSTATE MANUFACTURING CO., INC
123 Main Street, Newtown, Pennsylvania

	By
Secretary	Title
Louis V. Thompson	John J. McClerman President

(SEAL)

Dated_____

ACCEPTED:

L. F. DOMMERICH & CO., INC.

By_____
          Title

Dated_____

SECRETARY'S CERTIFICATE

RESOLVED, that the President, Vice-President, Secretary, Treasurer or other officer or any agent of this corporation, or any one or more of them, be and they are hereby authorized and empowered to enter into and execute on behalf of the corporation an agreement with L. F. Dommerich & Co., Inc. and/or its subsidiary, L. F. Dommerich & Co. California Corp. (hereinafter called the "Factor") relating to the pledge, assignment, negotiation and guarantee to said Factor of accounts, notes, bills, acceptances and other forms of obligations, collectively referred to as "receivables", and/or relating to the consignment, pledge, mortgage or other hypothecation of any merchandise or other property, now or hereafter belonging to or acquired by the corporation, to or with said Factor, and from time to time to modify or supplement said agreement and to make and modify, or supplement arrangements with said Factor as to the terms or conditions on which such receivables are to be pledged, assigned, negotiated or guaranteed to said Factor, and as to the terms or conditions on which merchandise or other property, now or hereafter belonging to or acquired by the corporation, may be consigned, pledged, mortgaged or otherwise hypothecated to or with said Factor, and they and each of them and any person or persons hereafter and from time to time designated by any of them to act for this Corporation are hereby further authorized and empowered from time to time to assign, transfer, deliver, endorse, negotiate or otherwise transfer and/or guarantee to said Factor and its assigns any and all receivables now or hereafter belonging to or acquired by the corporation, and for said purposes to execute and deliver any and all assignments, schedules, transfers, endorsements, contracts, guarantees, agreements or other instruments in respect thereof and to make remittances and payments in respect thereof by checks, drafts or otherwise, and they are further authorized and empowered from time to time to consign, designate, pledge, mortgage or otherwise hypothecate to or with said Factor merchandise or other property now or hereafter belonging to or acquired by the corporation, and for said purposes to execute and deliver any and all consignments, designations, schedules, mortgages, agreements, instruments of pledge and/or other instruments in respect thereof, and to do and perform all such other acts and things deemed by such officer or agent necessary, convenient or proper to carry out, modify or supplement any such agreement and arrangements made with said Factor, hereby ratifying, approving and confirming all that any of said officers or agents have done or may do in the premises.

I, Louis V. Thompson _____, do hereby certify that I am the

____ of Midstate Manufacturing Co., Inc. _____

a corporation organized and existing under and by virtue of the laws of the State of Pennsylvania ____, having its principal

business in the City of Newtown ____; that I am the keeper of the corporate records and the seal of said corporation; that the foregoing is a true, and correct copy of a resolution duly adopted and ratified at a special meeting of the Board of Directors of said corporation duly convened and held in accordance with its by-laws and the laws of said State at the office of said corporation

in the City of Newtown ____ State of Pennsylvania ____, on the_____day of

_____, 19 66 , as taken and transcribed by me from the minutes of said meeting and compared by me with the original of said resolution recorded in said minutes, and that the same has not in any way been modified, repealed or rescinded but is in full force and effect; that the within and foregoing agreement is the agreement referred to in said resolution and was duly executed pursuant thereto.

I do further certify that the following are the names and specimen signatures of the officers and agents of said corporation, so empowered and authorized, namely:

John J. McClernan (Print name) _____ (Signature)

President _____ (Print name) _____ (Signature)

Edward W. Granton (Print name) _____ (Signature)

Vice-President _____ (Print name) _____ (Signature)

Louis V. Thompson (Print name) _____ (Signature)

Treasurer _____ (Print name) _____ (Signature)

Thomas Goldstone (Print name) _____ (Signature)

Dan O'Reilly (Print name) _____ (Signature)

Witness my hand and seal of said corporation this_____day of_____, 19____

Corporate
Seal   _____.
(Secretary of said corporation)

GUARANTY

L. F. DOMMERICH & CO., INC.
485 Fifth Avenue
New York 17, New York

DEAR SIRS:

In order to induce you to enter into the within and foregoing agreement effective as of November 30   1966
Midstate Manufacturing Co., Inc., 123 Main Street, Newtown, Pennsylvania

(hereinafter referred to as the "client") and/or to continue under or to refrain at this time from terminating your present arrangeme
the client and in consideration of your so doing and/or in consideration of any loans, advances, payments, extensions of credit, benefits o
cial accommodations heretofore or hereafter made, granted or extended by you or which you have or will become obligated to make, g
extend to or for the account of the client whether under said agreement or otherwise, and/or in consideration of any obligation heret
hereafter incurred by the client to you whether under said agreement or otherwise, the undersigned (and each of them if more th
agree to be, without deduction by reason of setoff, defense, or counterclaim of the client, jointly and severally primarily liable to you for
performance of all the client's contracts and agreements with you, both present and future and any and all subsequent renewals, co
tions, modifications, supplements and amendments thereof, and for the payment to you of any and all sums which may be presently d
owing or which shall in the future become due and owing to you from the client. This liability shall include but not be limited
and all amounts charged or chargeable to the account of the client and any and all obligations incurred and sums due or to beco
to you, whether by way of overdraft or otherwise, under the aforementioned agreement and any other contract or agreement a
renewals, continuations, modifications, supplements and amendments thereof, as well as any and all other obligations incurred and othe
due or to become due to you, whether or not such obligations or indebtedness shall arise under any contract or agreement or shall be
sented by or payable under instruments of indebtedness or shall be acquired by you from any concern which is your parent or subsi
for which you may now or in the future act as factor; and in addition the undersigned shall be liable to you for attorneys' fees equal t
of the unpaid indebtedness and obligations of the client to you, if any claim hereunder is referred to an attorney for collection. All s
any time to the credit of the undersigned and any property of the undersigned at any time in your possession shall be deemed held
as security for any and all of the undersigned's obligations to you and to any company or companies which may now or at any time l
subsidiary, no matter how or when arising and whether under this or any other instrument, agreement or otherwise. Any and all prese
future debts and obligations of client to the undersigned are hereby waived and postponed in favor of, and subordinated to the fu
ment and performance of, all present and future debts and obligations of client to you. The undersigned hereby waive notice of acce
hereof and all notices and demands of any kind to which the undersigned may be entitled, including without limitation all dema
payment on, and notice of non-payment, protest and dishonor to the undersigned, or the client, or the makers, or endorsers of any i
other instruments for which the undersigned are or may be liable hereunder. The undersigned further waive notice of and hereby
to any agreement or arrangements whatever with the client or anyone else, including without limitation agreements and arrangeme
payment, extension, subordination, composition, arrangement, discharge or release of the whole or any part of said obligations or
indebtedness, contracts or agreements or other guarantors, or for the change or surrender of any or all security, or for compromise, v
by way of acceptance of part payment or of returns of merchandise or of dividends or in any other way whatsoever, and the same
no way impair the undersigned's liability hereunder. The undersigned shall have no right of subrogation, reimbursement or indemnity
soever and no right of recourse to or with respect to any assets or property of the client or to any collateral for the debts and obliga
the client to you, unless and until all said debts and obligations shall have been paid in full. Nothing shall discharge or satisfy the
of the undersigned hereunder except the full performance and payment of the said obligation and indebtedness with interest. The
signed agree that if the client or any of the undersigned should at any time become insolvent, or make a general assignment, or if a
in bankruptcy or any insolvency or reorganization proceeding shall be filed or commenced by, against or in respect of the client or
the undersigned, any and all obligations of the undersigned shall, at your option, forthwith become due and payable without notic
books and records showing the account between you and the client shall be admissible in evidence in any action or proceeding, s
binding upon the undersigned for the purpose of establishing the items therein set forth, and shall constitute prima facie proof thereof
that your monthly statements rendered to client shall, to the extent to which no objection is made within thirty days after date there
stitute an account stated between you and the client and binding upon the undersigned. This instrument is a continuing guaranty
shall remain in full force and effect and shall not be terminable so long as either the aforementioned agreement or your present arrar
with the client or any renewals, continuations, modifications, supplements and amendments of either thereof shall remain in force an
Thereafter this instrument shall continue in full force and effect until terminated by the actual receipt by you by registered or certifi
of written notice of termination from the undersigned or from the legal representative of any deceased undersigned; such terminati
be applicable only to transactions having their inception thereafter, and rights and obligations arising out of transactions having thei
tion prior to such termination shall not be affected. The death of any one or more of the undersigned shall not effect a terminatio
instrument as to such deceased or any of the surviving undersigned, nor shall termination by any one or more of the undersigned aff
continuing liability hereunder of such of the undersigned as do not give due notice of termination. The obligations hereunder sh
stitute primary and not secondary obligations. The undersigned to hereby waive any and all right to a trial by jury in any action
ceeding based hereon. This instrument cannot be changed or terminated orally, shall be interpreted according to the laws of the
New York, shall be binding upon the heirs, executors, administrators, successors and assigns of the undersigned and shall enure
benefit of your successors and assigns. Throughout this Guaranty, in referring to "you" it shall mean and include your subsidiar
Dommerich & Co. California Corp.

Witness:_____

Dated:_____

John J. McClernan (Signature of Guarantor)

_____
(Address)

Witness:_____

Dated:_____

Louis V. Thompson (Signature of Guarantor)

_____
(Address)

Witness:_____

Dated:_____

Howard W. Granton (Signature of Guarantor)

_____
(Address)

About the Author

IRWIN NAITOVE is a vice president of Chemical Bank New York Trust Co. and executive director of the bank's Dommerich Division. Before joining L. F. Dommerich & Co., Inc., then an independent factoring company, Mr. Naitove was vice president of Naitove Factors Corporation. He has lectured extensively on factoring and commercial financing to bankers and executives in many industries, and has served a foreign bank as adviser on American business practices and credit evaluation.